ITALIAN

GRAMMAR MADE EASY

A Comprehensive Workbook To Learn
Italian Grammar For Beginners
(Audio Included)

Lingo Mastery

ISBN: 978-1-951949-81-5

Copyright © 2024 by Lingo Mastery

CONTENTS

PREFACE
ABOUT THE LANGUAGE

The Italian language comes from ancient Latin, but not the classical one. When we talk about "classical" Latin, we refer to the language spoken by Cicero, Julius Caesar, Augustus, and all the most famous writers, philosophers and emperors that lived during the time of the Roman Empire.

In fact, the development of the Italian language started after the fall of the Roman Empire, in the fifth century CE, with the beginning of a new era: *the Middle Ages*, or **il Medioevo,** in Italian.

From that century, the so-called vulgar language — coming from the Latin **volgo**, *the people,* hence the language spoken by the people — started to spread across modern Europe. This is the reason why European languages such as Spanish, French, Portuguese, and Romanian share so many similarities. They all have the same roots, represented by vulgar Latin.

However, we would have to wait until the thirteenth century to see more written documents in Italian. Think of Dante, who started writing his **Divina Commedia** at the beginning of the fourteenth century.

 FUN FACT:

In Italy, people are still debating who speaks the "real" Italian. Of course, people from Tuscany claim that "award", as Dante wrote the Divine Comedy in Tuscan dialect.

Before publishing the final copy of his masterpiece *The Betrothed* — **I Promessi Sposi** — the famous Italian author Alessandro Manzoni said that he wanted to go to Florence to *rinse the clothes in the Arno River*, meaning that he wanted to review and correct the language used in the book according to the Tuscan dialect.

Just a fun fact: this workbook was written by a Lingo Mastery team member from Tuscany!

However, coming back to the present, over sixty million people all over the world speak Italian. Furthermore, over three million speak Italian as their second language. As expected, most of these Italian speakers live in Italy, but there are huge communities of Italians in South America, especially in Argentina, Venezuela and Brazil, in North America — because of the migrations in the last century — and in Croatia, Slovenia and Albania.

Each one of Italy's twenty regions has its own dialect, which were created by the influence of the several waves of invasions that prevailed in the different areas. The farther south we go, the stronger the dialect is. In some regions, the dialect mainly consists of a different accent and the use of words that are not that common in other regions.

However, if you speak the "standard" Italian, you will be understood everywhere in Italy. And if someone speaks a specific dialect with you, just ask them to switch to standard Italian. People are always willing to help, and they will appreciate the effort you are making by speaking with them in Italian.

And do not forget the hand gestures! These are part of the language, and you will find out that they are also very helpful to express yourself.

Finally, with this book, you will learn to master this wonderful language and to appreciate the Italian culture as well.

STRUCTURE

Learning a language is always challenging, but it should also be a fun and rewarding experience. The aim of this book is to offer you a self-taught course that will allow you to understand the language's grammar, as well as the culture to which it belongs.

This book will provide you with the linguistic, cultural and strategic tools to communicate in Italian. The thematic progression has been carefully planned so that the student can gain a more personal experience while practicing the language, using relevant situations.

Each chapter is dedicated to a specific topic that is required for fluency in Italian. We will focus on the most important ones, so that you can have all the tools you need to start navigating this fascinating language. The exercises following each section are designed to reinforce what has been learned while expanding your vocabulary.

Ready to start learning while having fun?

Iniziamo! *Let's start!*

INTRODUCTION

Far from being an exhaustive guide to the Italian language, with this book we want to give you the tools you need to start speaking and understanding the Italian language right away.

Of course, the first rule is the following: **take your time** while exploring the different sections — do not rush through them, but rather enjoy this journey into the Italian language.

This book is aimed at people of all ages who wish to start learning Italian, or people who have already studied the language but want to refresh their skills. It will cover the basics of levels A1–A2 in the Common European Framework of Reference for Languages (CEFR).

We want to give you the tools you need to build your knowledge and improve your skills.

Try completing all the exercises, as they are structured not only to make you practice what you are learning in that given section, but also to consolidate words and rules throughout the whole book.

In order to keep you motivated, we've included a few sections with some Italian tongue twisters — **scioglilingua** — or other fun expressions. They will not only enrich your vocabulary and give you the chance to speak like a native, but will also provide you with insight into Italian culture.

For the same reason, we added an extra chapter, which will address the main situations you may encounter when traveling to Italy. Feeling stressed before a trip to Italy? Not anymore. Now you will know what to do and what to say!

If anything, learn from the Italians: **go with the flow**, enjoy simple things, and take a break whenever you feel overwhelmed!

Ce la puoi fare e ce la farai!

You can do it, and you will do it!

HOW TO GET THE AUDIO FILES

Some of the exercises throughout this book come with accompanying audio files.
You can download these audio files if you head over to
www.lingomastery.com/italian-gme-audio

If you're having trouble downloading the audio, contact us at
www.lingomastery.com/contact

UNIT 1
BASIC CONCEPTS

CHAPTER 1
LEARNING HOW TO READ

We are not at school, but the starting point of this book is the alphabet. How so?

Well, you will be surprised to find out that you can write and read in Italian after learning the alphabet. Yes! Reading and writing in Italian is not that difficult. And this is because every letter has a specific sound — Italians pronounce every single letter of each word.

As an example, in English, we do not read every single letter in the word *"because"*. We read the letter *b* as we pronounce it in the alphabet, same for the letter *e,* but then we have *au* which has a completely different sound from that of the individual letters. Besides that, we do not pronounce the final *e.*

If the same word were read in Italian, we would read it as *beh-kah-oo-se,* as in Italian, all letters need to be pronounced and have their individual sound. Do not worry: it will be clearer once you learn the sounds of the Italian letters.

First things first: the Italian alphabet is made up of 21 letters, 16 consonants — **le consonanti** — and 5 vowels — **le vocali**.

Without further hesitation, let's delve into the Italian alphabet!

LETTER	NAME	PRONUNCIATION OF THE NAME	AS IN...
A	A	ah	**asino** (ah-sea-noh) *donkey*
B	Bi	bee	**bussare** (boo-sah-reh) *to knock*
C	Ci	chi (when followed by vowels i-e) k (when followed by vowels a-o-u)	**cereali** (che-reh-ah-lee) *cereal* **campana** (kahm-pah-nah) *bell*
D	Di	dee	**denaro** (deh-nah-roh) *money*
E	E	eh	**erba** (ehr-bah) *grass*

F	Effe	ehf-feh	**felice** (feh-lee-che) *happy*
G	Gi	gee (when followed by vowels i-e) gh (when followed by vowels a-o-u)	**giacca** (je-ah-kah) *jacket* **gonna** (gohn-nah) *skirt*
H	Acca	[-] no sound	**hotel** (oh-tehl) *hotel*
I	I	e	**isola** (ee-soh-lah) *island*
L	Elle	ehl-leh	**lumaca** (loo-mah-kah) *snail*
M	Emme	ehm-meh	**menta** (mehn-tah) *mint*
N	Enne	ehn-neh	**naso** (nah-soh) *nose*
O	O	oh	**oro** (oh-roh) *gold*
P	Pi	pea	**pentola** (pehn-toh-lah) *pot*
Q	Qu	qoo	**quadro** (coo-ah-droh) *painting*
R	Erre	ehr-reh	**regalo** (reh-gah-loh) *gift*
S	Esse	ehs-seh	**sale** (sah-leh) *salt*
T	Ti	tee	**tappeto** (tahp-peh-toh) *carpet*
U	U	oo	**uovo** (oo-oh-voh) *egg*
V	Vi Vu	vee voo	**vero** (veh-roh) *true/right*
Z	Zeta	dzeh-tah	**zucca** (dzoo-kah) *pumpkin*

 TRAP ALERT! Probably, the most difficult letters, both for English speakers learning Italian and for Italian speakers learning English, are *e* and *i*. Keep in mind that if you read the letter *e* as you do in English, you will say *i* in Italian.

You may have noticed that some letters are missing, some letters which are quite common and used in English! In fact, the letters J, K, W, Y, X are not part of the Italian alphabet. When you see them in Italian, it means that people are using a foreign or international word.

It is important for you to learn their sounds also, because it is possible that you have one of those letters in your first name or last name. If you have to say your name in Italy, for example to book a table or a hotel room, they will probably ask you to spell it.

LETTER	NAME	PRONUNCIATION OF THE NAME	AS IN...
J	i lunga	ee loon-gah	**jeans, jazz** (jee-ns, jah-dz)
K	kappa	kah-pah	**kiwi, karaoke** (kee-we, kah-rah-oh-keh)
W	doppia vu	doh-pea-ah voo	**wafer, windsurf** (vah-ph-ehr, windsurf)
X	ics	eeks	**xilofono** (xee-loh-phoh-noh)
Y	ipsilon	ee-psee-lohn	**yogurt, yacht** (yòh-goo-rt, yòht)

Now you know!

Of course, there are a few exceptions. And when we talk about exceptions, we are referring to a few combinations of letters having a specific sound. However, there are not many and they are summarized in the table below.

GROUP OF SOUNDS	PRONUNCIATION	AS IN...
SCI	she	**scivolo** (she-voh-loh) *slide*
SCE	scheh	**pesce** (peh-scheh) *fish*
GN	ñ	**campagna** (kahm-pah-ñah) *countryside*
GL	ll	**aglio** (ah-ll-e-oh) *garlic*

It all sounds quite easy, doesn't it?

Of course, when talking to an Italian speaker, they will tend to speak fast, so you may miss one or two letters. The vocabulary you have learned will help you understand better, but, in any case, do not be afraid to ask people to repeat their sentence or to speak more slowly.

Può ripetere, per favore?   *Can you repeat, please?*

Può parlare più lentamente?   *Could you speak more slowly?*

When writing, the most difficult thing will probably be understanding if and where you have to place an accent or a double consonant. Well, unfortunately, there is not much you can do. You will have to train your listening skills and try to learn as much vocabulary as possible. It will become easier with time and practice.

Starting with the accents, the good news is that Italian words can have a written accent only on the final vowel. You will never EVER find an accent right in the middle of a word, like in French, for example. Once again, you will have to know that word to know whether it has an accent or not.

However, when you write, it is very important to write that accent, because your word could acquire a completely different meaning without it. Let us show you a few examples:

papa	*pope*	VS	**papà**	*dad*
da	*from*	VS	**dà**	*he/she/it gives*
e	*and*	VS	**è**	*he/she/it is*
se	*if*	VS	**sé**	*oneself*
meta	*goal*	VS	**metà**	*half*
onesta	*honest*	VS	**onestà**	*honesty*
unita	*united*	VS	**unità**	*unity/unit*

These are just a few examples, but they show you why it is important, when you learn a new Italian word, to learn how to write it as well. Long story short: *accents are important!*

The same applies to double letters. We know that — especially when you have just started learning the language — the difference between a word with a double letter and the same word without that double letter may be very subtle, if not impossible to hear.

As we have done with the accents, let us show you a few examples of words whose meaning changes if you double one of the consonants.

papa	*pope*	VS	**pappa**	*baby food/dog food*
peli	*body hair*	VS	**pelli**	*leather (pl.)*
tori	*bulls*	VS	**torri**	*towers*
coro	*choir*	VS	**corro**	*I run*
spesa	*shopping*	VS	**spessa**	*thick*
tono	*volume*	VS	**tonno**	*tuna*
nono	*ninth*	VS	**nonno**	*grandfather*
sete	*thirst*	VS	**sette**	*seven*
casa	*home*	VS	**cassa**	*cash register*
caro	*dear*	VS	**carro**	*chariot*
sono	*I am*	VS	**sonno**	*sleep*
sano	*healthy*	VS	**sanno**	*they know*

Once again, this is the reason why it is important to build your own vocabulary. You should write down every new word you learn, so that you can see where to place those double letters. It will also help you train your listening skills. Do not despair — it will get easier with practice and time!

 **EXERCISES I**

1. Scrivi la pronuncia delle seguenti parole. *Write the pronunciation of the following words.*

Example: **letto**   *leht-toh*

- lampadina   _____

- televisione   _____

- cuscino   _____

- zanzara   _____

- radio   _____

- albero   _____

- verdure   _____

- gnomo   _____

2. Ascolta l'audio e scrivi le parole. *Listen to the audio file and write the words. Beware! There may be words with accents and/or double consonants. (Find audio on page 5.)*

- _____

- _____

- _____

- _____

- _____

- _____

- _____

- _____

- _____

CHAPTER 2
SUBJECT PRONOUNS & VERBS

Now you know how to read and spell in Italian, so what is the next step?

Obviously, now you have to learn how to start building your sentences! And the first thing you need to know is how the subject pronouns and the verbs work in Italian.

Let's start with the subject pronouns. In the table below, you will find the English ones along with their Italian translations.

SUBJECT PRONOUNS	PRONOMI PERSONALI SOGGETTO
I	io
you	tu
he/she/it	lui/lei/Lei
we	noi
you (pl)	voi
they	loro

Before talking about the use of subject pronouns in Italian, let's focus on the main differences from the English ones. First: The subject pronoun *I* — **io** — does not require a capital letter as in English.

Second: There are two different subject pronouns for *you* singular and *you* plural — **tu** and **voi**, respectively.

Third: You can see that, for the third person singular, there are three subject pronouns in Italian and three in English, but beware! There is an important difference. **Lui** corresponds to *he*, and

lei corresponds to *she*, but what about that **Lei** with a capital letter? Does it correspond to the subject pronoun *it*?

The answer is no. In Italian, there is no specific subject pronoun for things and animals. You will just pick one of the other two — **lui** or **lei** — according to the gender of the thing/animal you are talking about.

The subject pronoun **Lei** is not the same as *she*. It means *you* — singular — but in a <u>formal</u> way. To explain it better, you will have to conjugate the verb according to the subject pronoun Lei when you talk to someone you do not know, someone who is older than you, or is in a higher position than you — for example, your boss. Please note that the gender of the person does not matter; if you want to be formal, the subject pronoun to use is still Lei.

We know that it may be confusing at first, but it is very important to remember to be formal when needed. Of course, it all depends on the people you are talking to, but some may get offended if you are addressing them by using the simple **tu** and not the formal **Lei** if you do not know them.

Moving forward, when do we need the subject pronouns? Every time we build a sentence, you may answer. *But no!* Once again, the Italian language will surprise you.

As you know, in English, subject pronouns need to be explicated—that is, explicitly stated. In Italian, instead, it is quite the opposite. The subject pronouns are often omitted. Why, though?

The explanation is easy. In English, we require the explicated subject pronoun simply because the verb alone might be confusing. Let's assume someone tells you *Swim in the pool*. Who is this person talking about? Themselves? Them and a friend? Someone else? We cannot answer because the conjugated verb in the present tense is the same for the subject pronouns *I, you, we, you (pl), they*.

On the other hand, in Italian, the conjugated verb is different for each subject pronoun, thus allowing us to understand immediately about whom the speaker is talking. Using the subject pronoun, then, would just be a repetition.

If we take the example above, let's assume someone told you **'nuotano nella piscina'.** This sentence makes perfect sense and is not confusing at all, just because the conjugated verb **nuotano** is associated only with the subject pronoun *they* — **loro**. There is simply no need to specify it, as it is already clear who the speaker is talking about.

Keep in mind that adding the subject pronoun in an Italian sentence is not a mistake — it is just unnecessary most of the time. There are some instances where we do include the pronoun, especially when we want to emphasize the subject of a sentence.

Now you understand why Italian speakers LOVE English grammar when it comes to verb conjugation. It is much easier, as the conjugated verb rarely changes. But this is also why they often forget to specify the subject while talking in English — it is hard to get rid of a habit!

Let's move on to discuss the verbs. The infinitive of a verb is called **infinito** in Italian — yes, the same word means *infinity* as well, maybe because there are infinite verbs in the Italian language? Who knows.

How can you tell the difference between an **infinito** and a **verbo coniugato —** *a conjugated verb*?

That is easy. Italian verbs are grouped into three categories, each one with a very specific ending for its infinitive:

- **-are.** Examples: **lavare** *to wash*, **studiare** *to study*, **nuotare** *to swim*, etc.

- **-ere.** Examples: **prendere** *to take*, **vedere** *to see*, **vendere** *to sell*, etc.

- **-ire.** Examples: **mentire** *to lie*, **capire** *to understand*, **sentire** *to hear,* etc.

If you see a verb ending with **-are/ere/ire**, you are looking at at an infinitive.

There is an exception, though — *reflexive verbs*. To refresh your memory, reflexive verbs are used to express an action done to oneself, meaning that the **subject** — the person or object performing the action expressed by the verb — and the **object** — the person or object receiving the action — are **the same**. Example: *Dario is washing himself* — the subject and the object of that action are both Dario. Please note that some verbs, which are not reflexive in English, could be reflexive in Italian.

Reflexive verbs do belong to the -are/ere/ire groups, but they have an additional ending: **-si**. Let's break down some of them:

prepararsi	*to get ready*	**preparare+si**
offendersi	*to get offended*	**offendere+si**
vestirsi	*to get dressed*	**vestire+si**

You can see that the base form of reflexive verbs is similar to the **infinito** of all the other verbs, with the exception of that final **-si** which requires the elimination of the last vowel of the -are/-ere/-ire ending.

Now you know how to recognize the infinitive of all verbs, but what happens when that verb is conjugated?

In Italian, the conjugated verb is made of the **verb root + the ending** that corresponds to the related subject pronoun and the verb tense we intend to use.

The verb root is the verb without the -are/ere/ire ending. Let's use a previous example with the verb to swim, **nuotare**. In that example, the conjugated verb was **nuotano**. The infinitive is **nuotare,** so it is a verb belonging to the -are group. The verb root is **nuot-**, and the ending is **-ano**, which is the ending for the subject pronoun *they* — **loro —** in the simple present.

As for the verb position, in general you will find it at the beginning of the sentence, as the subject is only rarely expressed.

Examples:

Abito a Londra con i miei genitori.   *I live in London with my parents.*

The infinitive of **abito** is **abitare.**

Prendiamo un panino per pranzo.   *We take a sandwich for lunch.*

The infinitive of **prendiamo** is **prendere**.

Quando parti per le vacanze?   *When do you go on holiday?*

The infinitive of **parti** is **partire**.

 **EXERCISES II**

1. **Scrivi la traduzione dei pronomi personali soggetto in italiano.** *Write the translation of the subject pronouns in Italian.*

ENGLISH	ITALIANO
I	
you	
he/she	
we	
you (pl)	
they	

2. **Scrivi la radice dei verbi seguenti.** *Write the root of the following verbs. Beware! There may be reflexive verbs too.*

   Example: dormire _____**dorm-**_____

   - saltare _____ *to jump*

   - capirsi _____ *to understand each other*

   - lanciare _____ *to throw*

   - scegliere _____ *to choose*

   - comprare _____ *to buy*

   - radere _____ *to shave*

   - salutare _____ *to greet*

   - condire _____ *to season*

   - lamentarsi _____ *to complain*

CHAPTER 3
NOUNS

We will now focus on Italian nouns. First of all, how can you recognize a noun?

Well, as in English, a noun is often preceded by a definite or an indefinite article. Would you like a spoiler? No, it is better to let you discover the magical world of Italian articles in the next unit. You read it right. Articles, plural — very plural. More about them later.

Italian nouns. When it comes to nouns, the most difficult thing is probably not so much spotting them in a sentence, but knowing whether they are masculine or feminine nouns, singular or plural. That's because Italian nouns can have up to <u>four</u> different forms.

Do not worry, though. We will guide you and tell you a few tricks to navigate them. Please note that the following are just guidelines! There may be a few exceptions. This is the reason why we recommend, once again, to write down every new word you learn, along with its gender.

MASCULINE SINGULAR NOUNS	EXAMPLES
Most nouns ending with -o	**divano** *sofa*, **letto** *bed*, **parco** *park*
Days of the week (except for Sunday)	**lunedì** *Monday*, **martedì** *Tuesday*, etc.
Months	**gennaio** *January*, **febbraio** *February*, etc.
English words	**computer, smartphone, golf**

Useful info:

· Masculine nouns ending with **-o** will have a plural ending with **-i**.

  Examples: corpo-corpi *body-bodies*, **gatto-gatti** *cat-cats*, **libro-libri** *book-books*, **etc.**

· The only feminine word among the days of the week is Sunday — **domenica!**

· Also, if you are using an English word in Italian, please note that it will remain the same in its plural form. You do not have to add the final -*s* as required in English.

  Example: 1 computer, 2 computer   *1 computer, 2 computers*

FEMININE SINGULAR NOUNS	EXAMPLES
Most nouns ending with -a	**cartella** *folder*, **borsa** *bag*, **pesca** *peach*
Singular nouns ending with -i	**crisi** *crisis*, **tesi** *thesis*, **sintesi** *summary*
Nouns ending with -tù/tà	**gioventù** *youth*, **università** *university*

Useful info:

- Feminine nouns ending with **-a** will have a plural ending with **-e**.

- **Examples: partita-partite** *match-matches*, **bottiglia-bottiglie** *bottle-bottles*, **cucina-cucine** *kitchen-kitchens*, etc.

- Names of islands are generally feminine: **Sardegna, Sicilia**, etc.

There are also some singular nouns ending with **-e**, but unfortunately they can be either masculine or feminine. You do not have a choice: you will have to learn those nouns in order to know their gender.

Examples: ape (fem. sing.) *bee*, **mare** (masc. sing.) *sea*, **pane** (masc. sing.) *bread*, **lezione** (fem. sing.) *lesson*, etc.

Note: When reading something in Italian, it may happen that you see an asterisk at the end of a word, like in **ragazz***. What does it mean, though? The asterisk is used to refer to a group of people, no matter their gender, and it has become quite common to avoid any gender bias.

 **EXERCISES III**

1. **Sottolinea i nomi nel testo seguente.** *Underline the nouns in the following text.*

Mi chiamo Marco e sono un insegnante di francese. Lavoro al liceo da dieci anni. Insegnare è la passione della mia vita, anche se da bambino sognavo di diventare un attore famoso! Nel mio tempo libero mi piace viaggiare ed esplorare dei posti nuovi, visitare musei, e andare ai concerti.

My name is Marco and I am a French teacher. I have been working in a high school for ten years. Teaching is my life's passion, even if I dreamed of becoming a famous actor when I was a child! In my free time, I like traveling and exploring new places, visiting museums, and going to concerts.

2. **Maschile o femminile? Singolare o plurale?** *In the table below, put an X to mark whether the following nouns are masculine or feminine, singular or plural.*

	MASCHILE	FEMMINILE	SINGOLARE	PLURALE
tavolo				
piedi				
salotto				
zebra				
zie				
scanner				
martedì				
vanità				
biglie				
cane				

CHAPTER 4
QUALIFYING ADJECTIVES

Next step: *the adjectives!* But how would you define an adjective?

Well, a qualifying adjective is a word describing a noun, telling us something more about it. For example, *an interesting book about Italian grammar*. *Interesting* is our adjective, and it gives us additional information about this amazing book! Yes, *amazing* is another adjective that we could use to describe it.

In English, qualifying adjectives precede the noun they refer to. In Italian, in general it is quite the opposite. You will normally find the adjective after the noun. However, in most cases, placing the adjective before the noun is not considered a mistake. It is just less common.

Examples:

Una ragazza divertente	*A funny girl*
Una bella casa	*A beautiful house*
Un amico timido	*A shy friend*

Bad news, my friend. Their position is not the difficult thing about Italian adjectives. Unfortunately, once again, English grammar has spoiled us. In fact, in English, adjectives are invariable, meaning that they never change. They can refer to a masculine or a feminine noun, a singular or a plural one, but they will always remain the same.

Well, in Italian, adjectives must match the gender and the number of the noun they refer to. In most cases, then, Italian nouns have four different forms: masculine singular (MS), feminine singular (FS), masculine plural (MP), and feminine plural (FP). Some of them are 'kinder', and just have two, one for the singular form and the other for the plural.

Just as nouns can have up to four different endings so too can adjectives. The only thing that will change — in most cases — is the final letter. Do you remember when we told you how to recognize masculine and feminine nouns in the previous chapter?

Let's look at a few examples:

MS	FS	MP	FP
piccolo *small*	**piccola** *small*	**piccoli** *small*	**piccole** *small*
grande *big*	**grande** *big*	**grandi** *big*	**grandi** *big*
comodo *comfortable*	**comoda** *comfortable*	**comodi** *comfortable*	**comode** *comfortable*

Maybe you have already figured out how it works. In the adjectives with the four forms, you can see that the final letter changes according to the "signature vowel" of the gender. As we have already mentioned in the previous chapter, the ending **-o** is more common for masculine singular nouns, **-a** for feminine singular ones, **-i** for masculine plural nouns, and **-e** for feminine plural ones. The same thing applies to adjectives.

There are also adjectives with two forms only (**grande**). You can see that this adjective does not change according to gender, but according to its number only. Adjectives ending with the letter **-e** have two forms — one for the singular and one for the plural — and not four.

It is not that difficult, but — especially when you have just started learning Italian — you will have to make an effort to remind yourself that your adjective has to agree with the noun it describes. Once again, practice makes perfect, and, most importantly, do not forget that **sbagliando si impara —** *you learn by making mistakes.*

 **EXERCISES IV**

1. **Come ti descriveresti? E come descriveresti un amico o un'amica?** *How would you describe yourself? And how would you describe a friend of yours? Use the adjectives below to create your first two descriptions, but do not forget to adapt them according to the subject!*

alto (tall) – basso (short) – divertente (funny) – timido (shy) – estroverso (outgoing) – generoso (kind) – noioso (boring) – ambizioso (ambitious) – giovane (young) – vecchio (old) – pigro (lazy) – attivo (active)

Sono_____

_____

_____

I am...

È_____

_____

_____

He/She is...

2. **Scrivi le diverse forme degli aggettivi sotto.** *Fill in the table below with the missing forms of the following adjectives.*

MS	FS	MP	FP
	verde		
		brutti	
tranquillo			
			brave

CHAPTER 5
ADVERBS

L'avverbio — the adverb — is another important element in a sentence. But how would you define it, and what is the difference from an adjective?

As we have seen in the previous chapter, an adjective refers to a noun, and it tells us something more about it. On the other hand, an adverb refers to a verb or an adjective, and not to a noun.

Examples:

- *I woke up late this morning. Late* is the adverb, and it refers to the action of *waking up.*

- *It is very cold in the house. Very* is the adverb, and it refers to the adjective *cold.*

In English, adverbs can often be formed by adding the suffix *-ly* to the base form of the adjective. Think about *slow-slowly, loud-loudly, extreme-extremely*, etc.

The corresponding suffix in Italian would be **-mente**. We will do the same as we have just done in English; we will form an adverb starting from an adjective:

AGGETTIVO	AVVERBIO
sicuro *sure*	**sicuramente** *surely*
veloce *quick*	**velocemente** *quickly*
vero *true*	**veramente** *truly*
gentile *kind*	**gentilmente** *kindly*

A few tricks to create your own adverbs, when possible:

- The suffix **-mente** is added to the feminine form of the adjective
  (see example above, **sicuro-sicuramente**).

- If the adjective ends in **-le** or **-re**, we lose the final **-e** when we add the suffix
  (e.g., **gentile-gentilmente**).

- If the adjective ends in **-e**, you can simply add **-mente** (e.g., **veloce-velocemente**).

Unfortunately, not all adjectives have a corresponding adverb with the -mente suffix. As you may expect, there are irregular adverbs as well.

We have compiled a short list for you with the most common and useful ones:

ancora	*still*	**già**	*already*
bene	*well*	**insieme**	*together*
contro	*against*	**mai**	*never*
dentro	*inside, in*	**male**	*badly*
dietro	*behind*	**sempre**	*always*
dopo	*afterward*	**spesso**	*often*
fuori	*outside, out*		

📝 EXERCISES V

🎧 **1. Ascolta l'audio.** *Listen to the audio file and fill in the gaps. (Find audio link on page 5.)*

Mio fratello ha avuto il suo _____ esame ieri. Si è svegliato _____ per

andare all'università con il bus ed è arrivato con trenta minuti di _____! Gli esami lo

rendono _____ molto _____ . Alla fine è andato _____! È

tornato a casa _____ e _____ di se stesso.

My brother had his last exam yesterday. He woke up very early to go to the university by bus and arrived thirty minutes early! Exams always make him very nervous. In the end, it went great! He came back home happy and proud of himself.

2. Crea l'avverbio. *Create the missing -mente adverbs in the table below by starting with the corresponding adjective.*

AGGETTIVO	AVVERBIO
rapido	
beato	
leale	
dolce	
regolare	

CHAPTER 6
SENTENCE TYPES

Last step before we move forward and start putting your new skills into practice!

With this chapter, we will focus on the different sentence types. First of all, which types of sentences are we going to talk about?

We will start with basics, which is learning how you can make affirmative and negative sentences, and questions.

You have already explored the different elements of an Italian sentence, and, if you put them all together, what you get is an affirmative sentence.

Let's start with a couple of examples:

- **Giulia guida la sua macchina nuova.**

  Giulia drives her new car.

  In this example, the subject — Giulia — is expressed because we have a given name, meaning that the subject of the sentence is not a generic *she*. After the subject, there is the conjugated verb, **guida**. The conjugated verb comes from **guidare,** the infinitive of a verb belonging to the **-are** group. Then we have the direct object — *What is Giulia driving? Her new car* — with an adjective as well. As already mentioned, the adjective often follows the noun it refers to.

- **Abbiamo visto sicuramente lo stesso film.**

  We surely watched the same movie.

  In this instance, the subject is not expressed, but in Italian, we know for sure that it corresponds to the subject pronoun **noi**, as it is related to the conjugated verb **abbiamo**. No other option is possible. We also have an adverb in this sentence, and we can recognize it thanks to the **-mente** ending.

We have seen two examples of affirmative sentences, but how can you make a negative one? For once, Italian grammar is actually easier than the English!

You can easily make a negative sentence by adding a **non** in front of the verb. It does not matter which verb or tense you are using. Just add that short word and the magic will happen: your affirmative sentence has become a negative one.

Same examples as above, but in negative sentences:

- **Giulia non guida la sua macchina nuova.**

  Giulia does not drive her new car.

- **Non abbiamo sicuramente visto lo stesso film.**

  We surely did not watch the same movie.

As you can see, the only difference is that **non** in front of the conjugated verb.

Now, moving on to questions. Fancy more good news? Well, to create a question, the only thing you have to do is adding a question mark at the end of your sentence.

Yes, you read that right. When you write a question, you just need to add a question mark at the end of your sentence. If you are asking a question, then you only need to work on your intonation.

Troppo bello per essere vero? *Too good to be true?*

Well, it is true. Let's take the examples of affirmative sentences above and turn them into questions:

- **Giulia guida la sua macchina nuova?**

  Is Giulia driving her new car?

- **Abbiamo visto lo stesso film?**

  Did we watch the same movie?

See? We were not lying ;)

📝 EXERCISES VI

1. Ascolta l'audio e scrivi le frasi. *Listen to the audio file and write the sentences. Beware! There will be affirmative and negative sentences, but also questions. (Find audio on page 5.)*

- _____

- _____

- _____

- _____

- _____

- _____

- _____

2. Trasforma le frasi seguenti in affermative (A), negative (N), o interrogative (?). *Transform the following sentences into affirmatives (A), negatives (N) or questions (?).*

- Siamo andati al mare lo scorso fine settimana. *We went to the seaside last weekend.*

  _____ (N)

- Prendo una bibita fresca? *Do I get a fresh drink?*

  _____ (A)

- Non mangia i latticini. *He/She doesn't eat dairy products.*

  _____ (?)

- Marco parte ogni estate con i suoi amici. *Marco goes away every summer with his friends.*

  _____ (N)

- Hai visto la luna stasera? *Have you seen the moon tonight?*

  _____ (A)

- Preferiscono il mare alla piscina. *They prefer the sea to the swimming pool.*

  _____ (?)

EXTRA
TONGUE TWISTERS!

You have done an excellent job so far, so you deserve a fun break! And what is more fun than a few tongue twisters... in Italian?

First, a disclaimer. The following tongue twisters are difficult to read for Italian speakers as well. Actually, you may even find some of them easier than they would be for an Italian speaker. They play with the sound of letters or with the repetition of similar words.

Buon divertimento. Have fun with your first two... which are also going to be the easiest ones *evil laugh*.

- **A quest'ora il questore in questura non c'è.**

Our first tongue twister plays with the repetition of the letters **que**. It is translated as *At this time, the police chief is not at the police headquarters.*

Pronunciation: *ah coo-eh-stoh-rah eel coo-eh-stoh-reh een coo-eh-stoo-rah nohn chè.*

- **Sereno è, seren sarà. E se non sarà sereno, si rasserenerà.**

Okay, this one is about the weather and, as you can see, it involves a lot of *s*. Its translation is *It is clear, it will be clear. And if it's not clear, it will get clear.* The tongue twister of the optimist who has already planned a weekend out of town and has just seen the weather forecast announcing a storm for those two days.

UNIT 2

FIRST STEPS

CHAPTER 1
CARDINAL NUMBERS

Okay, what do you need if you are planning a trip to Italy, or just want to be able to have a conversation in Italian?

I numeri — *The numbers!*

Numbers are <u>everywhere</u> in our daily conversation. Whether you want to tell someone your age, or you just want to understand the price of something you want to buy, you need to learn the numbers.

In this chapter, we will focus on cardinal numbers. What are cardinal numbers?

Well, one, two, three... These are cardinal numbers. We will show you how to count in Italian, and you will be surprised to find out that it is not that difficult.

In fact, just like in English, the most "difficult" part is to count from 1 to 19, as in this range numbers are all irregular. Then, from 20 on, once you learn how to add the units to the tens, you are set to go.

Let's start with those irregular ones, then. **Iniziamo!**

0	zero	5	cinque	10	dieci	15	quindici
1	uno	6	sei	11	undici	16	sedici
2	due	7	sette	12	dodici	17	diciassette
3	tre	8	otto	13	tredici	18	diciotto
4	quattro	9	nove	14	quattordici	19	diciannove

Well, with these numbers, you do not have any other option but to learn them by heart. Keep in mind the pronunciation guidelines we provided at the beginning of this book. For example, do not be tempted to read **zero** like you would in English. Remember that it should be read as *dzeh-roh*, as the letter *e* in Italian is read as *eh*. If you read it as *zeero*, in Italian you would write it as **ziro.**

Same for the number 11. Do not fall into temptation and say *unodieci* — literally, one-ten — as it does not mean anything in Italian. As already mentioned, numbers from 1 to 20 are irregular and do not follow any rules. *Sorry.*

Now that you have learned those numbers, before adding the tens to the equation, let us give you an example of how easy it is to count from 20 on. Let's count from 20 to 29.

20	venti	25	venticinque
21	ventuno	26	ventisei
22	ventidue	27	ventisette
23	ventitré	28	ventotto
24	ventiquattro	29	ventinove

That looks easier, doesn't it?

Because it is. After number 19, numbers become regular, just like in English. Think about it: *Twenty-one, twenty-two, twenty-three...*

Well, in Italian there are still a couple of things we need to mention. Specifically, about numbers 21, 23, and 28. Have you noticed something peculiar about them?

Let's start with number 21. If it were a completely regular number, it would be **ventiuno**. We would keep the final *i* of **venti**. However, that little vowel has disappeared. Final result: **ventuno**. Keep it in mind, as this rule will apply to the following tens as well.

Moving on to number 23. Is there anything weird about it? Well, kind of. Did you see the final accent? Yes, even though number 3 does not have any accent — **tre** — when we have the tens with it, we must add that final accent.

Finally, if you take a look at number 28, you will soon realize that the same rule with number 21 applies here as well. This number is not **ventiotto**, but **ventotto**. Once again, we have deleted the *i* of **venti**.

Now you know how to count! The last numbers you need to learn, then, are the tens.

30	trenta	70	settanta
40	quaranta	80	ottanta
50	cinquanta	90	novanta
60	sessanta	100	cento

How does it work from 100 on, then? It is easy. 200 is **duecento,** 300 is **trecento,** 400 is **quattrocento,** etc.

Examples:

462: **quattrocentosessantadue.** If we break down this super long word, this is what we get: **quattro-cento-sessanta-due**.

833: **ottocentotrentatré.** Do not forget the accent on the three when it comes with a ten!

We know that you are looking forward to learning more, so why not add numbers from 1000 on?

In Italian, 1000 is translated as **mille**. When you use it, make sure to pronounce that double consonant. But keep in mind that the sound of that double does not correspond to the Spanish *ll*. A double *l* in Italian just gives a longer sound to that consonant, not a different one.

However, what happens when we want to say a number like 2000, 3000, or more? Well, that **mille** becomes **mila.** Then counting becomes very regular.

Examples: duemila, tremila, quattromila, cinquemila, etc.

Useful words/expressions related to numbers:

Quanto/quanta/quanti/quante...? Translated as *how much/how many*, their difference is not related to singular/plural only. The right form of **quant*** will have to agree in number and gender with the thing you are talking about. **Quanto** is masculine singular, **quanta** is feminine singular, **quanti** is masculine plural, and **quante** is feminine plural.

Examples:

Quanti figli hai?   *How many sons/children do you have?*

Quanto gelato hai mangiato?   *How much ice cream did you eat?*

Quanto costa/costano...? This question corresponds to *How much is/are...?* The difference is that, in Italian, you will have to say **quanto costa** if you are asking the price of just one item, while **quanto costano** must be used when you are asking for the price of several items, or for one in its plural form.

Examples:

Quanto costa quella maglietta? *How much is that T-shirt?*

Quanto costano le patatine fritte? *How much are the fries?*

Quanto costano quei pantaloni? *How much are those trousers?*

Quanti anni hai? This is the question you should ask to find out someone's age. Please note that, in Italian, we must use the verb *to have*. The Italian question is literally translated as *How many years do you have?* Funny, right? But this is why Italians struggle when asking or telling someone's age. They tend to use the verb *to have*, and not *to be*. The same applies for English speakers learning Italian, obviously!

As per the answer, sometimes you could use the little word "ne" ("ne" in bold). It can replace direct object pronouns when referring to a number or a quantity adjective.

Examples:

Quanti fratelli hai? *How many siblings have you got?*

Ho tre fratelli. / Ne ho 3. *I have three siblings.*

 CULTURAL TIP: Never ask for a woman's age, especially if she looks more than 40 years old. In fact, it may sound rude. If you ask that question, they'll probably reply **Non si chiede l'età a una donna!** *You never ask for a lady's age!*

Well, with that last tip, this chapter is over, and now you are ready to buy both a gelato and a whole apartment, too! **Niente più scuse!** *No more excuses!*

 **EXERCISES I**

1. Scrivi i numeri in italiano. *Write the following numbers in Italian.*

- 35 _____
- 72 _____
- 33 _____
- 91 _____
- 58 _____

- 3 _____
- 246 _____
- 999 _____
- 1320 _____
- 9021 _____

2. Rispondi alle seguenti domande usando i numeri. *Answer the following questions using numbers in Italian.*

- Quanti fratelli hai? *How many siblings do you have?*

_____

- Quanto costa un biglietto al cinema? *How much is a movie ticket?*

_____

- Quante pagine ha questo libro? *How many pages long is this book?*

_____

- Quanti anni hai? *How old are you?*

_____

- In che anno siamo? *What year is it?*

_____

CHAPTER 2
ORDINAL NUMBERS

Yes, there is still something to say about numbers. Does the definition of ordinal numbers ring a bell?

Probably so. Ordinal numbers are used to indicate the order of things in a set. For example, *the first, the second, the third*, etc.

It is important to learn how to say them in Italian too, as they can be very useful. And we know that you do not want to stop while talking in Italian just because you do not know how to translate those words, right? *RIGHT?*

So, how can we build these other numbers? Even ordinal numbers are irregular until the 10th. Afterwards, they become regular and very easy to form.

Their use is the same as in English, and they are preceded by the definite article. However — you knew that a *however* was coming — in Italian there are several forms of definite articles.

We will not get into details right now, as we will dedicate a whole chapter to Italian definite articles, but for now just know that the ordinal number has to agree with number and gender with the noun it refers to. More about that in a bit.

The only difference in terms of use concerns the days. In Italian, when you are saying the date, you must not use ordinal numbers, but the cardinal ones. In short, you do not say *it is the 10th*, for example, but just *it is the 10* — **è il 10.**

Once again, for the first ordinal numbers, you have no other option but to learn them by heart –they are all irregular.

1st	primo/prima/primi/prime
2nd	secondo/a/i/e
3rd	terzo/a/i/e
4th	quarto/a/i/e
5th	quinto/a/i/e
6th	sesto/a/i/e
7th	settimo/a/i/e
8th	ottavo/a/i/e
9th	nono/a/i/e
10th	decimo/a/i/e

As you can see, we have four options for each ordinal number. For example, **primo** is masculine singular, **prima** is feminine singular, **primi** masculine plural, and **prime** feminine plural. We know, the idea of having to think about number and gender all the time is annoying, but it will become easier with time and practice.

Now, what happens after the 10th? Well, ordinal numbers become very regular. You will have to take the cardinal number, take the last vowel off and pick one of the endings among **-esimo/a/i/e.** When the unit of the cardinal number is a 3, the *e* will double.

Examples:

12th **dodicesimo/a/i/e** (dodici+esim*)

27th **ventisettesimo/a/i/e** (ventisette+esim*)

143rd **centoquarantatreesimo/a/i/e** (centoquarantatré+esim*)

E così via... *And so on...*

EXERCISES II

1. Scrivi i numeri ordinali in italiano. *Write the ordinal numbers in Italian. Beware! Write the right form as indicated (MS-Masculine Singular, FS-Feminine Singular, MP-Masculine Plural, FP-Feminine Plural).*

- 42nd   _____   MS

- 13th   _____   MP

- 33rd   _____   FS

- 191st   _____   FP

- 1st   _____   MP

- 9th   _____   FP

- 71st   _____   MS

- 10th   _____   FS

2. Ascolta l'audio. *Listen to the audio file and fill in the gaps.*

Ieri ho partecipato alla mia _____ gara di scherma! È stata un'esperienza

_____ . Mi allenavo da_____ anni per questo momento. Non

sono arrivato _____ , ma _____ . Sono stato comunque molto

orgoglioso del mio _____ . C'erano _____ atleti in gara!

Translation

Yesterday I took part in my first fencing competition! It has been a wonderful experience. I had been training for five years for this moment. I did not come first, but ninth. I am still very proud of my result. There were forty athletes in the competition!

CHAPTER 3
DEFINITE AND INDEFINITE ARTICLES

It is now time to dive into the world of Italian articles. Are you ready to learn something new and challenge yourself?

First, we should briefly discuss the difference between definite and indefinite articles — **gli articoli determinativi e indeterminativi**. We use them every day, but maybe you do not remember their definition. Let's refresh your memory.

In English, there is just one definite article: *The*. This definite article is used before something we know about. For example, if someone says *the house,* the reader or the other speaker knows which house they are referring to.

As for the indefinite articles, the identity of the noun is not known, or maybe it is just a generic one. In English, we have two indefinite articles: *a/an*. We use the former in front of nouns beginning with a consonant, and the latter before nouns starting with a vowel. For example, if we say *a house,* we do not know which specific house the speaker is talking about.

Now that we have clarified the difference between definite/indefinite articles, it is time to talk about Italian articles. Let's start with the definite ones.

In Italian, there are seven definite articles. Yes, you read it right. S-E-V-E-N. Once again, this is the reason why Italians like English grammar. One definite article versus seven. Not that bad, right?

Definite articles are often perceived as one of the most difficult things to learn, but it is not because they are complicated — it is just because there are a lot of them. You will have to take your time to learn them, and practice, practice, practice. That is truly the only secret to mastering them.

Yes, definite articles may be annoying — and there are undoubtedly a lot — but the good news is that they follow a few strict rules. Once you learn those rules, it is just a matter of practice — and making mistakes.

The first step that will allow you to put those rules into practice, though, is knowing whether the noun you intend to use is masculine, feminine, singular or plural. If you want to refresh your memory before delving into the articles, take a look at the chapter where we discussed the differences among nouns and gave you a few tricks to identify them.

Which are the Italian definite articles, then? We will present them in different groups.

For masculine nouns:

- **IL**: To be used before most masculine singular nouns beginning with a consonant. Its plural form is **I**.

  Examples: il letto – i letti *the bed – the beds,* **il telefono – i telefoni** *the phone – the phones,* **il cane – i cani,** *the dog – the dogs,* etc. When switching to the plural, do not forget to change the ending of the noun as well.

- **LO**: Yes, another definite article for masculine singular nouns. However, **lo** is used for very specific nouns: those beginning with **s+consonant, i+vowel, gn, pn, ps, z, y, x.** Its plural form is **GLI**.

  Examples: lo stivale – gli stivali *the boot – the boots,* **lo psicologo – gli psicologi** *the psychologist – the psychologists,* **lo zaino – gli zaini** *the backpack – the backpacks,* etc.

For feminine nouns:

- **LA:** Do not worry. This is the only one in this group. **La** is used in front of all feminine singular nouns beginning with a consonant. Its plural form is **LE**.

  Examples: la finestra – le finestre *the window – the windows,* **la forchetta – le forchette** *the fork – the forks,* **la partita – le partite** *the match – the matches,* etc.

For masculine and feminine nouns beginning with a vowel:

- **L'**: This definite article is used in front of all singular nouns beginning with a vowel, no matter their gender. However, when we switch to the plural form of those nouns, we will have to differentiate them according to their gender. If the noun is a masculine one, the definite article for the plural will be **GLI**. If it is feminine, the corresponding definite article will be **LE**. Please note that, when you have the definite article with the apostrophe, the following noun is attached to it — there is no space between article and noun.

Examples: l'ape – le api *the bee – the bees,* **l'elefante – gli elefanti** *the elephant – the elephants,* **l'orso – gli orsi** *the bear – the bears,* etc.

So yes, the Italian definite articles are numerous, but, as you have just seen, they follow a few strict rules and — most importantly — there are no exceptions! Probably, at the beginning, the masculine definite articles may be the most confusing ones — as you have five options in total between singular and plural forms — but trust us: you will overcome this challenge and your Italian skills will get stronger than ever!

Now, moving on to the indefinite articles. Do not worry: the indefinite articles are far fewer than the definite ones. Well, "only" four of them. Of course, just like in English, they only have a singular form. Let's take a look at them.

For masculine nouns:

- **UN**: It corresponds to the definite article **IL.**

  Examples: un palazzo – il palazzo *a building – the building,* **un cantante – il cantante** *a singer – the singer,* **un cuscino – il cuscino** *a pillow – the pillow,* etc.

- **UNO**: It corresponds to the definite article **LO** – the same rules apply to this indefinite article as well.

  Examples: uno yacht – lo yacht *a yacht – the yacht,* **uno gnomo – lo gnomo** *a gnome – the gnome,* **uno spazio – lo spazio** *a space-the space,* etc.

For feminine nouns:

- **UNA**: It corresponds to the definite article **LA.**

  Examples: una cucina – la cucina *a kitchen – the kitchen,* **una gita – la gita** *a trip – the trip,* **una lampada – la lampada** *a lamp – the lamp,* etc.

For nouns beginning with a vowel:

- **UN**: Same indefinite article as the one we have seen for masculine nouns. We use it in front of masculine nouns beginning with a vowel. It corresponds to the definite article **L'**.

Examples: **un albero** – **l'albero** *a tree – the tree*, **un evento** – **l'evento** *an event – the event*, **un occhio** – **l'occhio** *an eye – the eye*, etc.

- **UN':** It is used in front of feminine nouns beginning with a vowel. Do not forget that apostrophe! It corresponds to the definite article **L'**. Once again, between the indefinite article and the following noun, there is no space, because there is an apostrophe.

  Examples: **un'estate** – **l'estate** *a summer – the summer*, **un'alba** – **l'alba** *a sunrise – the sunrise*, **un'isola** – **l'isola** *an island – the island*, etc.

In general, Italian learners find the indefinite articles easier than the definite ones... Maybe because there are fewer differences among them?

In any case, this is everything you should know about Italian articles! We are aware that it is a lot to process and learn. Once again, do not rush. You will not learn them in ten minutes, and you will not learn them in a week. This is definitely a topic requiring time, as articles are used more in Italian than in English.

Ma non ci sono dubbi: ce la farai! *But there is no doubt: you will make it!*

Let's start practicing with a few exercises. Do not worry, you will have the chance to practice Italian articles in the next chapter too. Sorry, not sorry!

✎ EXERCISES III

1. Completa la tabella con gli articoli determinativi. *Fill in the table with the missing forms of the Italian definite articles.*

SING.	PLUR.
IL	
LO	
	LE
L'	

2. Aggiungi il giusto articolo determinativo. *Add the right definite article for the following nouns.*

- _____ barca (f. sing.)
- _____ divano (m. sing.)
- _____ angoli (m. plur.)
- _____ aereo (m. sing.)
- _____ epoca (f. sing.)

- _____ vittorie (f. plur.)
- _____ scoglio (m. sing.)
- _____ zuccheri (m. plur.)
- _____ artiste (f. plur.)

3. Aggiungi il giusto articolo indeterminativo. *Add the right indefinite article for the following nouns.*

- _____ aperitivo (m.)
- _____ fiore (m.)
- _____ malattia (f.)
- _____ esperienza (f.)
- _____ stadio (m.)

CHAPTER 4
POSSESSIVE ADJECTIVES

As their name suggests, possessive adjectives — **gli aggettivi possessivi —** are used to express ownership or possession. Examples of possessive adjectives in English are *my, your, his, her,* etc.

In English, as well as in Italian, possessive adjectives are placed in front of the noun they refer to. They never replace it, because otherwise they would become a possessive pronoun — like *mine, yours,* etc.

As you may expect, there are a few differences between Italian and English possessive adjectives. First important difference: Italian possessive adjectives must agree in gender and number with the noun they refer to. It is exactly what happens with all the other adjectives.

Each possessive adjective has four different forms, shown in the table below.

	MS	FS	MP	FP
my	mio	mia	miei	mie
your	tuo	tua	tuoi	tue
his/her/its	suo	sua	suoi	sue
our	nostro	nostra	nostri	nostre
your	vostro	vostra	vostri	vostre
their	loro	loro	loro	loro

When you look at the Italian possessive adjectives, the first thing you may notice is that the four options are not that different from one another. Well, it would be so much easier if they were invariable like in English, but we do enjoy a bit of a challenge, right?

One of the first things you may have noticed is that, for *he/she/it*, we have only one possessive adjective, and not three different ones for each subject pronoun.

Another change is the ending of the possessive. And this ending is rather similar to the ones for the other adjectives. For example, we have **-o** for the masculine singular form, **-a** for the feminine singular one, **-i** for the masculine plural and **-e** for the feminine plural.

An important thing to remember: the possessive adjective needs to match the gender and the number of the noun it refers to — the object of possession — and not that of the owner.

Before showing you some examples of sentences with possessive adjectives, we must tell you another important difference with the English ones. We have already highlighted the importance of definite articles in Italian, and now you will understand this better.

In fact, in Italian, possessive adjectives must be preceded by the definite article. In short, you do not say *my car*, but you would say *the my car*. It sounds quite weird in English, doesn't it?

Now you can also understand the importance of the article when using **loro** as a possessive adjective. If you take another look at the table above, you can see that it is invariable. The four forms are exactly the same — **loro, loro, loro, loro**. The only thing that will change, then, is the definite article in front of it.

We know what you are thinking. Yes, the definite article must be chosen according to the gender and number of the possessive adjective — as it precedes that word, and not the main noun.

Exception alert: Just to make things more fun, there is an exception to the use of definite articles with possessive adjectives. In front of possessive adjectives related to close family members, we must not use the definite article. But it is not over: this rule applies when that family member is in its singular form only. If it becomes plural, then it needs the definite article.

To explain it better, in Italian you would say *my brother* just like you would in English, but if you have more than one brother, then you will have to say *the my brothers*. Yeah, we know, it's a bit weird.

Exception to the exception: sorry, but there is another thing to mention. Now we know that singular family members do not need the definite article, but... well, sometimes they do. Family members in their singular form must have the definite article when there is another adjective after the possessive one. For example, *my dear mother* should be translated as *the my dear mother*, as there are two adjectives: the possessive one, and *dear*.

Let's look at a few examples now:

- **La mia cena era deliziosa.**   *My dinner was delicious.*

Here we have the full set of *definite article+possessive+noun*. We should start with the main noun: **cena** is a feminine singular noun, so the corresponding possessive adjective is **mia** (see table above). The definite article used in front of feminine singular nouns is **la**.

- **I loro gatti sono molto divertenti.**   *Their cats are very funny.*

In this instance, the main noun is **gatti**, which is a masculine plural one. The corresponding possessive adjective is **loro**, and the definite article is **i**. Do not think about **gli** when we have possessive adjectives: in fact, there are no possessive adjectives beginning with a vowel, nor beginning with all those letters requiring **lo** in their singular form. When it comes to masculine words, then, you have only two options for the definite article: **il** for the singular, **i** for the plural.

- **Mia sorella lavora come insegnante.**   *My sister works as a teacher.*

Here the main noun is **sorella**, which is a feminine singular noun. The possessive adjective for feminine singular noun, once again, is **mia**. We must not add the definite article before the possessive adjective, as this is a close family member. However, in the event of several sisters working as teachers, he/she would say **Le mie sorelle lavorano come insegnanti.** When switching to the plural form of close family members, the definite article is required, and in this instance, we would need the feminine plural one, **le**.

> Silvia, la tua maglietta è molto bella.

> Grazie Giulio! Anche il tuo cappello è molto bello!

Congratulazioni! *Congratulations!* You have just finished this chapter about possessive adjectives. Well, you have finished the part about grammar. To finish it properly, here is a list of family members in Italian.

madre/mamma	*mother/mom*	**sorella**	*sister*
padre/papà	*father/dad*	**sorellastra**	*stepsister*
patrigno	*stepfather*	**fratelli**	*siblings*
matrigna	*stepmother*	**zio**	*uncle*
genitori	*parents*	**zia**	*aunt*
moglie	*wife*	**cugino**	*cousin (m)*
marito	*husband*	**cugina**	*cousin (f)*
figlio	*son*	**nonno**	*grandfather*
figlia	*daughter*	**nonna**	*grandmother*
fratello	*brother*	**nipote**	*nephew/niece**
fratellastro	*stepbrother*		

An important thing to highlight– a nasty false friend. In Italian, the word **parenti** does not mean *parents*. As shown above, the translation of *parents* is **genitori**. On the other hand, **parenti** means *relatives*.

Also, as you may have noticed, in Italian there are two different words for cousin according to the gender of that cousin — **cugino/cugina**. However, there is no difference between *nephew/niece*, which is always translated as **nipote.** To clarify the gender of that person, you will have to look at the definite article — **il nipote,** masculine, or **la nipote,** feminine.

* The word **nipote** is also used to refer to grandson and granddaughter!

 **EXERCISES IV**

1. Completa la tabella con le forme mancanti. *Fill in the table with the missing forms of the Italian possessive adjectives.*

	MS	FS	MP	FP
my	mio			mie
your		tua		
his/her/its				
our	nostro		nostri	
your			vostri	vostre
their				

2. Traduci le seguenti parole. *Translate the following words related to family members along with the possessive adjective and the definite article — if needed. If there is more than one option, write them all.*

- My brother   _____

- Their sons   _____

- Our father   _____

- Your niece   _____

- My sisters   _____

- His aunt   _____

- Their uncles   _____

- Your cousin   _____

3. Ascolta l'audio. *Listen to the audio file and add the missing words.*

La _____ famiglia è molto grande! Ho tre _____ e due

_____, sette _____ e quattordici _____. Ci riuniamo

sempre per _____ e ci divertiamo sempre tantissimo. I _____ genitori

hanno lavorato sodo per supportarci, e ora spero di poter fare lo stesso con _____.

CHAPTER 5
PRONOUNS

Now it is time to tackle the different kinds of pronouns we have in Italian. We must use that plural — *pronouns* — as there are many, just like in English.

Good news, though. You are already familiar with some of them — the subject pronouns, for example, **i pronomi personali soggetto!** These pronouns are *I, you, he/she/it,* etc. You already know everything about them, so no need to use more space in this book. We'll just remind you that subject pronouns are generally not used in Italian when talking or writing.

- **I Pronomi Riflessivi**   *Reflexive Pronouns*

We have already mentioned reflexive verbs in our overview, but just as a reminder, we will say that reflexive verbs are those verbs whose subject and object are the same. Every reflexive verb requires a reflexive pronoun, otherwise it cannot be defined as such. *He washes himself,* for example. We have the verb (washes) and the reflexive pronoun (*himself*). Without the pronoun it (*He washes*), the verb is no longer a reflexive one.

It is time to discover the reflexive pronouns in Italian. And yes, the Italian ones are way shorter than the English ones.

MYSELF	mi
YOURSELF	ti
HIMSELF/HERSELF/ITSELF	si
OURSELVES	ci
YOURSELVES	vi
THEMSELVES	si

As you may have noticed, the reflexive pronoun for *he/she/it* and *they* is the same — **si**. As subject pronouns are not really used, you will understand understand about whom the speaker is talking by looking at the conjugated verb, which is going to be different according to the specific subject pronoun.

Examples: Mi preparo per la festa *I get ready for the party;* **Ci vestiamo e partiamo** *We get dressed and we leave;* **Vi lavate la mattina** *You wash yourselves in the morning.*

- **I Pronomi Personali Oggetto**   *Direct Object Pronouns*

Even though you may not be familiar with this definition, you are definitely familiar with these pronouns. Direct object pronouns answer the questions *Who? What?* and they replace the noun we would use to answer. For example, to say *You watch a movie,* we can also say *You watch it.* That *it* is a direct object pronoun.

Let's discover the Italian ones.

ME	mi
YOU	ti
HIM/HER/IT	lo/la
US	ci
YOU (PL)	vi
THEM	li/le

You can see that some of them are exactly the same as the reflexive ones — **mi, ti, ci, vi**. As per *him/her/it,* we have only two options, one for the masculine — **lo** — and the other for the feminine — **la**. As per *them,* we have two options because, once again, one is for the masculine — **li** — and the second is for the feminine — **le**.

An important difference from the English direct object pronouns is that the Italian ones do not follow the verb, they precede it.

Beware! When **lo** or **la** are followed by a vowel or an *h,* they will lose their own final vowel which will be replaced by an apostrophe. In short, they will become **l'**.

Examples: Ti ho visto ieri *I saw you yesterday;* **L'avevo vinta** *I had won it;* **Le incontro tutti i giorni** *I meet them every day,* etc.

Exception: When the verb is in its infinitive form, the direct object pronoun will be attached to the end of the verb, and the verb will lose its final vowel. **Example: Vado a prenderla (prendere+la)** *I'm going to get her.*

- **I Pronomi Oggetto Indiretto**   *Indirect Object Pronouns*

We are almost at the end, **coraggio!** We now know that direct object pronouns answer the questions *What? Who?* Well, indirect object pronouns answer the questions *To whom? To what?*

For example, if we say *They give him a book*, that *him* is an indirect object pronoun. *To whom do they give the book?* To him.

Indirect object pronouns exist in Italian as well. Let's take a look at them in the table below.

TO ME	mi
TO YOU	ti
TO HIM/HER/IT	gli/le
TO US	ci
TO YOU (PL)	vi
TO THEM	loro

Once again, we have some similarities with reflexive and direct object pronouns, such as **mi, ti, ci,** and **vi.**

There is an important difference for *to him/her*, though. We need to use **gli** as indirect object pronoun for the masculine — yes, just like the definite article — and **le** for the feminine — again, just like the definite article.

Moreover, in English, the indirect object pronoun is often introduced by the preposition *to*, and it goes after the verb. However, in Italian, the indirect object pronoun, in most cases, does not require a preposition; when the pronoun is required, it usually goes before the verb — except for **loro.**

Examples: Ho comprato loro una maglietta *I bought them a T-shirt;* **Le ho cantato una canzone** *I sang a song to her;* **Vi ho parlato** *I spoke to you,* etc.

Exception: Just like with direct object pronouns, whenever a verb is in its infinitive form, the indirect object pronoun will be attached to the end of the verb, and the verb will lose its final vowel. **Example: Vado a dargli (dare+gli) un regalo** *I'm going to give him a gift.*

- **I Pronomi Relativi**   *Relative Pronouns*

These are the last ones! Or rather, there are other Italian pronouns, but let's say that relative pronouns are the last useful ones you need to learn in order to improve your skills and vocabulary.

The purpose of relative pronouns is to create a "connection" between two sentences. If we say *She saw a friend that she knows very well,* the relative pronoun is *that* because it connects the two sentences — *she saw a friend* with *she knows very well.*

The most used relative pronoun in Italian is definitely **che.** And for once, in Italian, there are fewer options than in English! We can use **che** for *that, which,* and *who* — but beware! Only in affirmative or negative sentences, but not for questions.

Examples: Ho comprato una gonna che mi piace *I bought a skirt that I like;* **Hanno visto un film che sembra interessante** *They watched a movie which seems interesting;* **L'amica di Giulia, che ha 30 anni, vive qui** *Giulia's friend — who is 30 years old — lives here.*

 **EXERCISES V**

1. Che cos'è? *Take a look at the following pronouns, and write whether they are SP (Subject Pronouns), REF (Reflexive Pronouns,) DP (Direct Object Pronouns), IP (Indirect Object Pronouns), and/or RP (Relative Pronouns). If there is more than one option, write them all.*

- mi   _____

- lui   _____

- vi   _____

- le   _____

- la   _____

- che   _____

- si   _____

- lo   _____

2. Ascolta l'audio. *Listen to the audio file and add the missing words in the text that follows.*

Ti presento un amico _____ conosco da una vita, Luca! _____ ho conosciuto

durante una vacanza quando eravamo giovani. Da allora _____ siamo visti molte

volte. _____ è un tipo molto estroverso, _____, invece, sono molto

timido. _____ ho già parlato di sua moglie, Francesca, _____ lavora con

_____? Vorrei _____ un regalo per il suo compleanno.

Translation

I want to introduce a friend that I have known all my life, Luca! I met him during a holiday when we were young. Since then, we have seen each other several times. He is very outgoing, while I am very shy. Have I talked to you about his wife, Francesca, who works with him? I would like to give her a birthday present.

CHAPTER 6
PREPOSITIONS AND ARTICULATED PREPOSITIONS

Well... yes, we gave you a break from articles, but now it is time to talk about them one last time.

First, let us introduce the Italian prepositions. We use prepositions on a daily basis. Examples of English prepositions are *at, to, with, of...*

Luckily, there is not a big difference between English and Italian prepositions in terms of numbers, unlike the definite articles. And there is also not so much to say about them. The only thing you need to do is learn them and start using them... right away!

In the table below, you will find the Italian prepositions, along with their corresponding translations in English.

DI	*of/about*
A	*to (movement)/at*
DA	*by/from/at*
IN	*in*
CON	*with*
SU	*on*
PER	*to/for (purpose)*
TRA/FRA	*between/among*

See? We were not lying. Each Italian preposition has a corresponding one in English.

The most versatile preposition is probably **da,** which can be translated with a bunch of different English prepositions. Let's see its different meanings:

- Provenance: It is used to express someone's provenance.

  Example: Vengo da Milano, *I come from Milan.*

- From: It corresponds to the basic *from.*

  Example: Non voglio niente da lei, *I do not want anything from her.*

- From... to...: When paired with the preposition **a,** it can be translated as *from... to.*

  Example: Siamo aperti da lunedì a venerdì, *We are open from Monday to Friday.*

- Duration: It can be used both in questions and in affirmative/negative sentences to express the duration of an action. In English, we would use *since, how long, in, for...*

  Example: Non la vedo da una vita, *I have not seen her for ages.*

- When: It can be used in sentences — but not in questions — for expressions like *When I was a child,* etc.

  Example: Da adolescente, uscivo tutti i giorni, *When I was a teenager, I used to go out every day.*

Taking a closer look, you may think that **tra** corresponds to *between,* and **fra** to *among.* **Errore!** Quite simply, in Italian, there is no difference between those two English prepositions. Both **tra** and **fra** can mean *between* or *among.*

Example: Non ci sono ballerini tra (fra) i partecipanti, *There are no dancers among the participants.*

Let's look at a few examples of sentences with Italian prepositions:

Sono venuto per aiutarti.   *I came to help you.*

With this example, we can see the use of the preposition **per,** along with the direct object pronoun **ti.** We remind you that, when there is a verb in its infinitive form, the direct object pronoun does not precede the verb, but it literally follows it, just like the last carriage of a train ;)

Siamo da Marcello.   *We are at Marcello's.*

With this example, you can see another use of the Italian preposition **da**. We use it when we want to say *at someone's house/place*.

Before moving on to the articulated prepositions, there is another important thing to discuss, though: *phrasal verbs*.

Phrasal verbs are those verbs requiring a specific preposition right after them. For example, *get up, put in, throw away,* etc. In English, there is a HUGE number of them. This is the reason why Italian students always despair when their teacher gives them a list of the English phrasal verbs to learn by heart. It is a real nightmare for them!

In Italian, phrasal verbs exist, but do not worry — they are way fewer than in English. This is also why learning the English ones is so difficult for Italian speakers, especially when a verb means something completely different when followed by a certain preposition — think about all the possible translations of *get+preposition*!

In order to help you, we have compiled a short list of the most common phrasal verbs in Italian:

andare dietro (a)	*to follow/to court*
andare fuori	*to go out*
andare sotto	*to go under*
dare addosso a	*to criticize*
mettere addosso	*to put on*
mettere dentro	*to put in*
mettere sotto	*to put under*
mettere giù	*to put down*
portare avanti	*to get ahead*
mandare giù	*to swallow (figurative)*
tirare su	*to raise*
tirare avanti	*to survive*
tirarsi indietro	*to pull out*

Tirare avanti is probably the funniest phrasal verb in Italian. It means *to survive*. Well, there is another verb that literally means *to survive*, and it is **sopravvivere**, so it is not a phrasal verb. What is the difference between the two of them, then? In general, the verb **sopravvivere** is more common than **tirare avanti,** which is actually used to answer the question *How are you?* If you answer **Tiro avanti,** it is a sarcastic way to say that, despite everything, you are still alive.

Now, let's move on and discuss the articulated prepositions. An articulated preposition, as its name suggests, is the result of the combination between a definite article and a preposition.

If you think about it, prepositions are often followed by an article. For example, if we say *We go to the beach,* we have *to* and *the,* preposition and definite article, one right after the other. Sure, in English it is definitely easier because there is only one definite article — *the* — but what happens in Italian with its army of articles?

Well, in some cases things are just as easy as in English. The preposition is followed by a space, and then the chosen definite article. However, just to spice things up, most prepositions merge with definite articles, giving birth to what? To an articulated preposition!

Take a look at the table below to see what happens when prepositions and definite articles combine. But please, do not despair. It is easier than it seems.

	IL	LO	LA	L'	I	GLI	LE
DI	del	dello	della	dell'	dei	degli	delle
A	al	allo	alla	all'	ai	agli	alle
DA	dal	dallo	dalla	dall'	dai	dagli	dalle
IN	nel	nello	nella	nell'	nei	negli	nelle
CON	con il	con lo	con la	con l'	con i	con gli	con le
SU	sul	sullo	sulla	sull'	sui	sugli	sulle
PER	per il	per lo	per la	per l'	per i	per gli	per le
TRA/FRA	tra il	tra lo	tra la	tra l'	tra i	tra gli	tra le

Now take a deep breath. What has just happened? Well, you have just met the Italian articulated prepositions.

If you take a closer look, you realize that, in most cases, it is not that bad. Articulated prepositions look just like what they are: a mix between a preposition and a definite article. The only ones that truly change are those with **in** as the preposition. The others are not that bad, are they?

Also, you can see that the prepositions **con, per, tra/fra** do not merge with the definite articles. Please note that, even though in the table above we added examples with **tra** only, the same applies to **fra**. Remember: those two are totally interchangeable.

 FUN FACT

In terms of pronunciation, there is an important thing to highlight about the articulated preposition **nei**. We can all agree on the fact that this word should be pronounced as *neh-ee,* but it is important to stress that the first *e* should be a closed one (*é*), and not an open one (*è*). If you pronounce it as *nèh-ee,* then you will be saying *moles,* and not *in the!*

If you are thinking *Okay, whatever, I am just going to skip this section,* think twice. How many times do you use a preposition on its own while talking, and how many times do you use a preposition followed by a definite article? Now you know why it is important to learn the articulated prepositions and practice as much as you can.

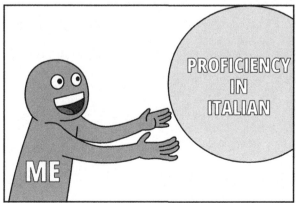

Important! The Saxon genitive ('s) does not exist in Italian. For example, in Italian, you cannot say *The lady's passport*. You will have to say *The passport of the lady*. The chances of you having to use the articulated prepositions, then, get higher and higher.

To finish this challenging chapter, let's look at a few examples of sentences with articulated prepositions:

- **Vado al mare ogni estate.**   *I go to the seaside every summer.*

In this sentence, we need an articulated preposition, just like in English — *to+the*. The articulated preposition is **al,** which is **a+il.** In fact, the noun **mare** is a masculine singular one.

- **Vengono dalla Spagna.**   *They come from Spain.*

This is an important use of the articulated prepositions in Italian. When you want to say which country you come from — but not the city — this will require a definite article. It is as if you were saying *They come from the Spain.* **Spagna** is a feminine country, therefore its definite article is **la.** As we said above, the preposition used to express someone's provenance is **da**, then **da+la=dalla.**

- **Mia cugina parte per il suo lavoro.**   *My cousin is leaving for her job.*

Here we have a combo! Articulated preposition and two possessive adjectives. We remind you that, in Italian, possessive adjectives must be preceded by the corresponding definite article — apart from times when we are we are talking about family members in their singular form, just like **mia cugina. Per** does not merge with the definite article, so the result of their union is simply **per il.**

EXERCISES VI

1. Completa la tabella. *Fill in the table below with the missing articulated prepositions.*

	IL	LO	LA	L'	I	GLI	LE
DI							
A							
DA							
IN							
CON							
SU							
PER							
TRA/FRA							

2. Completa le frasi. *Complete the following sentences with the right articulated prepositions. Use the English translation as a guide.*

- Francesca viene _____ Italia.

  Francesca comes from Italy.

- _____ sua città ci sono pochi supermercati.

  In his/her city, there are few supermarkets.

- Dove stai andando? _____ stazione!

  Where are you going? To the train station!

- La finestra è _____ televisione e la radio.

  The window is between the TV and the radio.

- Mi hanno parlato bene _____ professore.

  They spoke well about the professor.

- Mio padre è seduto _____ sedia.

  My father is sitting on the chair.

- Vi stavamo aspettando _____ cena pronta!

  We were waiting for you with the dinner ready!

- È molto dinamico _____ sua età.

  He is very active for his age.

EXTRA
TONGUE TWISTERS!

You knew that this section was coming... more Italian tongue twisters are waiting for you!

Daje tutta — a funny expression in the Roman dialect, which is used to encourage someone.

- **Tre tigri contro tre tigri.**

Let's start with a "basic" one. The translation of this tongue twister is *Three tigers versus three tigers.* It is difficult because of the alliterations within those words. You have the repetition of the consonants **tr**, which actually makes you want to add some more!

Pronunciation: *treh tee-gree kohn-troh treh tee-gree.*

- **Sopra la panca la capra campa, sotto la panca la capra crepa.**

Another tongue twister involving an animal. Well, in this instance it is quite a sad story. This tongue twister says *On the bench the goat is alive, under the bench the goat dies.* The hard part of this one is the last part of each sentence. You will see that it is quite difficult to pronounce **capra campa** and **capra crepa**, one word right after the other. That poor goat, though.

Pronunciation: *soh-prah lah pahn-kah lah kah-prah kahm-pah, soht-toh lah pahn-kah lah kah-prah kreh-pah.*

UNIT 3

BUILDING YOUR FIRST SENTENCES

CHAPTER 1
PRESENT TENSE

Are you ready to start building your first Italian sentences?

We will start from the basics, with the present tense — **il presente semplice**. Compared to the verb conjugation in English, it is obvious that it is going to be a little more complicated, but not impossible. In fact, conjugating a verb in English may seem even too easy! The verb is always the same, and the only thing you need to do is adding an *s* when using *he/she/it* as subject pronouns.

 FUN FACT

When you have too few rules, you are likely to forget them, and this is exactly what happens to Italian speakers when learning English. In fact, English conjugation is so repetitive that they often forget to do the only thing required for the third person singular! English teachers in Italy know that struggle *veeery* well.

As already explained, Italians do not use subject pronouns simply because the verb — when conjugated — changes its endings all the time, so there is no need to be repetitive and add the subject. Just looking at the verb, we already know who the subject of the sentence is.

Of course, just like in English, there are regular and irregular verbs. With regards to irregular verbs, you have no choice but to learn their conjugation by heart, whereas regular verbs are actually easier than you might think. There are specific rules for the conjugation of regular verbs.

Do you remember that, in Italian, we have three groups of verbs? The three groups ending with **-are, -ere** and **-ire**. Well, when you conjugate a regular verb, you need to take that ending off, and what you're left with is the *verb root*, which is the part of the verb without the ending of the infinitive.

Examples: cant- is the root of the verb **cantare** – *to sing;* **ball-** is the root of the verb **ballare** – *to dance;* **pens-** is the root of the verb **pensare** – *to think*, etc.

Once you have the verb root, you simply have to add the endings of the present tense to it, which are different for each subject pronoun. Let's look at three examples of regular verb conjugation in the present tense, one for each verb group.

	PARLARE *to talk*	VEDERE *to see*	SENTIRE *to hear*
io	parl-o	ved-o	sent-o
tu	parl-i	ved-i	sent-i
lui/lei/Lei	parl-a	ved-e	sent-e
noi	parl-iamo	ved-iamo	sent-iamo
voi	parl-ate	ved-ete	sent-ite
loro	parl-ano	ved-ono	sent-ono

That's it! You can see that each conjugated verb is made of two parts: the verb root and the specific ending of each subject pronoun. All endings are different. You can also see that there are not too many differences among the three groups. For example, the endings are the same across the three groups for the subject pronouns *I, you, we.*

And now you can also understand better why a subject pronoun is not needed when speaking in Italian. If someone says **parlate,** we know immediately that the subject of that sentence is **voi**. There is no other possibility.

The only possible confusion is with the third person singular, because if the subject pronoun isn't there, you may not know if it's a *he* or a *she*. However, in general you can easily figure it out from the context. If in doubt, just specify it. We remind you that using the subject pronoun is not a mistake — it is just not that common or necessary.

Also, do not forget to conjugate the verb according to **Lei** whenever you have to be formal, no matter the gender of the person you are talking to.

An important thing about pronunciation. English speakers tend to read the third person plural of **-are** verbs as **parl-àno**, as if there were an accent on the last *a*. However, the correct pronunciation is **pàrl-ano**.

Let's look at a few examples of sentences in the present tense:

- **Incontrano sempre persone nuove.** *They always meet new people.*

In this example, we know that the subject pronoun of the sentence is **loro,** as the conjugated verb is **incontr-ano**, which comes from the infinitive of the regular verb **incontrare,** *to meet.*

Also, another thing to highlight is the position of the adverb **sempre,** which in English precedes the verb in the present tense, while in Italian it follows it.

As for the position of the adjective, in this instance we could place **nuove** in front of the noun it refers to — **persone** — or after it, and there would be no difference.

- **Vendi il tuo appartamento?**   *Are you selling your apartment?*

Vendi is a conjugated verb coming from the infinitive of **vendere** — *to sell* — a verb belonging to the **-ere** group. The verb root is **vend-** and the ending of the present tense is **-i**, so we know that the subject of this sentence is **tu.** We also have a possessive adjective, so it is a great opportunity to refresh your memory and stress that, in Italian, possessive adjectives need the 'company' of a definite article.

- **Il fine settimana dormiamo fino alle dieci.**   *On the weekend, we sleep until 10 a.m.*

The verb of this sentence is **dormiamo,** a regular verb belonging to the **-ire** group. By now you know that the ending **-iamo** is used for the subject pronoun **noi.** Please note that we could place **il fine settimana** at the beginning or at the end of the sentence, and it would not make any difference.

Well, even regular verbs can feel a little bit adventurous. Quite a few verbs belonging to the **-ire** group, in fact, have a slightly different conjugation. Let's look at a couple of examples.

	CAPIRE *to understand*	**PREFERIRE** *to prefer*
io	cap-isc-o	prefer-isc-o
tu	cap-isc-i	prefer-isc-i
lui/lei/Lei	cap-isc-e	prefer-isc-e
noi	cap-iamo	prefer-iamo
voi	cap-ite	prefer-ite
loro	cap-isc-ono	prefer-isc-ono

See? Even though these verbs are considered regular ones, they require a few additional letters before the regular ending of the present tense — **-isc-**. This rule applies to the subject pronouns **io, tu, lui/lei/Lei, loro** only. In fact, the endings of **noi** and **voi** are completely regular, without any 'extra bits'.

Here's a short list of more **-ire** verbs with this particular conjugation:

agire (agisco)	*to act*
colpire (colpisco)	*to hit*
costruire (costruisco)	*to build*
finire (finisco)	*to finish*
gestire (gestisco)	*to manage/handle*
guarire (guarisco)	*to heal*
inserire (inserisco)	*to insert*
obbedire (obbedisco)	*to obey*
pulire (pulisco)	*to clean*

restituire (restituisco)	to give back
spedire (spedisco)	to send
suggerire (suggerisco)	to suggest

One last thing to say about regular verbs, we promise you! Whenever a verb has an infinitive ending with **-care** or **-gare**, you have to add something when conjugating it in order keep the hard sound of that **-c** or **-g**. First let's look at a couple of examples, and then we'll discuss them.

	PAGARE *to pay*	**CERCARE** *to look for*
io	pago	cerco
tu	paghi	cerchi
lui/lei/Lei	paga	cerca
noi	paghiamo	cerchiamo
voi	pagate	cercate
loro	pagano	cercano

As you can see, we have added an extra **h** to the verb ending for the subject pronouns **tu** and **noi.** Why, though? Well, the infinitive of the verb **pagare** is read as *pah-gah-reh,* so the letter **g** has a hard sound. **Pago** is read as *pah-goh.* However, if it were **tu pagi** — without the extra **h** — the verb would be pronounced as *pah-jee.* In order to keep the hard sound of the infinitive, we require that extra letter.

The same applies to the verb **cercare,** *cher-kah-reh.* If we said **tu cerci,** the pronunciation would become *cher-chi.* By adding the extra **h** for *you/we,* we keep the hard sound of the consonant.

Now, irregular verbs. Of course, we are not going to show you all the irregular verbs of the Italian language, just the main ones. And we feel like the first ones you should learn are definitely **to be** and **to have.** Let's discover their conjugation in the present tense.

	ESSERE *to be*	AVERE *to have*
io	sono	ho
tu	sei	hai
lui/lei/Lei	è	ha
noi	siamo	abbiamo
voi	siete	avete
loro	sono	hanno

Well, now you understand why these two are the kings of the irregular verbs!

If we take a look at **essere**, you can see how the verb changes throughout its conjugation.

A few things worth noticing:

- The conjugated verb for the subject pronouns **io** and **loro** is the same — **sono —** which is exceptional for Italian grammar. However, it is hard to get confused even when we do not use the subject pronoun.

- The conjugated verb for **tu — sei —** is written and pronounced just like number six.

- Do not forget the accent on **è!** That accent is very important, and it gives the letter an open sound. In fact, if you write it as **e**, or you pronounce it with a closed sound, you will be saying *and* instead of using the verb *to be.*

Now, let's move on to the verb **avere**, which is as weird as the verb *to be* when conjugated:

- You can see that the conjugated verb for the subject pronouns **io, tu, lui/lei/Lei,** and **loro** begins with an *h*. Even though it has no sound, that letter is as important as the accents! Why? Because without it, the verb changes its meaning: for example, **anno** means *year,* **ai** is an articulated preposition, **a** is a preposition...

- The only regular form of the verb is **avete!** In fact it has the regular verb root — **av-** — followed by the corresponding ending of the subject pronoun **voi.**

At the end of this book, you will find a few tables with the conjugation of the main irregular verbs in the present tense. Take a look at them, and try to learn them **a poco a poco** — *little by little.*

 **EXERCISES I**

1. Scrivi la base verbale. *Write the verb root of the following verbs.*

- partire   _____   *to leave*

- credere   _____   *to believe*

- comprare   _____   *to buy*

- vincere   _____   *to win*

- prendere   _____   *to take*

- scegliere   _____   *to choose*

- mentire   _____   *to lie*

2. Scrivi la coniugazione dei verbi regolari. *Write the conjugation of the regular verbs in the table below.*

	AMARE *to love*	PIANGERE *to cry*	FINIRE *to finish*
io			
tu			
lui/lei/Lei			
noi			
voi			
loro			

3. Aggiungi il verbo. *Add the missing verb in the following sentences. Beware! There may be some irregular verbs. Use the tables at the end of the book as a reference.*

- _____ sempre al mare a settembre. (andare, io)

  I always go to the seaside in September.

- _____ le migliori torte del mondo! (cucinare, lei)

  She makes the best cakes in the world!

- Quando _____ per l'Africa? (partire, tu)

  When do you leave for Africa?

- _____ casa tutti i giorni. (pulire, loro)

  They clean their house every day.

- _____ dagli Stati Uniti. (venire, noi)

  We come from the United States.

- Sig. Rossi, mi _____ il suo indirizzo, per favore? (scrivere, Lei)

  Mr. Rossi, could you write your address for me?

CHAPTER 2
REFLEXIVE AND RECIPROCAL VERBS

If you remember, we have already mentioned the reflexive verbs — **i verbi riflessivi** — twice. The first time, when we introduced the verbs in Italian. The second time, when we showed you the different types of Italian pronouns.

To refresh your memory, reflexive verbs are different from "ordinary" verbs because the subject and the object of the action expressed by the verb are the same. In short, the subject (singular or plural) is performing an action to itself. For example, *I asked myself a question*, or *They are driving themselves to work today.*

There is another group of verbs, though, which is rather similar to the reflexive group. We are talking about reciprocal verbs — **i verbi reciproci.** What is the difference from reflexive verbs? It is an easy one. Reciprocal verbs are used to describe an action performed by two or more people on each other. For example, *You two often wrote to each other; They hugged each other,* etc.

Now that you know all about these verbs — for real! — it is time to learn how to use them. Do not worry, though. Their conjugation is basically the same as that of all the other verbs.

The first thing you need to do, as usual, is to take the verb root. However, we remind you that the infinitive of reflexive and reciprocal verbs is slightly different. The infinitive will not end with **-are, -ere,** or **-ire**, but with **-si**. We also remind you that the -si ending is just an extra addition; all these verbs belong to the -are, -ere, or –ire groups, so you will just have to see what comes before the reflexive/reciprocal ending. For example, **ricordarsi (ricordare+si), perdersi (perdere+si), pentirsi (pentire+si)**.

When you want to conjugate a reflexive or a reciprocal verb, then, you will have to take the endings **-arsi, -ersi, -irsi** off in order to find the verb root. After that, well, you will have to conjugate the verb as discussed in the previous chapter.

However, you're not done yet, as you'll also need to remember to add the corresponding reflexive pronoun. Think about it: if you say *Do you mind pouring yourself a drink?* You are using a reflexive verb with a reflexive pronoun. However, if you forget to add that pronoun, the question becomes *Do you mind pouring a drink?* You are not using a reflexive verb anymore, and the meaning of the sentence has changed accordingly.

An important difference, compared to English, is that the reflexive pronoun precedes the verb it refers to, and does not follow it. We recommend revising the reflexive pronouns before checking the conjugation of reflexive and reciprocal verbs. Good news! They may have a different definition, but the conjugation of these two groups of verbs is the same.

What do you need to do, then? Take the reflexive pronoun, then the verb root, and add the endings of the simple present that you have learned in the previous chapter. **Ecco fatto!** *That's it!*

Take a look at the conjugation of three reflexive verbs in the table below, one for each verb group (**-arsi, -ersi, -irsi**).

	CHIAMARSI *to be named*	DECIDERSI A *to decide to*	VESTIRSI *to get dressed*
io	mi chiamo	mi decido	mi vesto
tu	ti chiami	ti decidi	ti vesti
lui/lei/Lei	si chiama	si decide	si veste
noi	ci chiamiamo	ci decidiamo	ci vestiamo
voi	vi chiamate	vi decidete	vi vestite
loro	si chiamano	si decidono	si vestono

See? The conjugation of these verbs is just like with regular *-are, -ere* and *-ire* verbs. Of course, if an "ordinary" verb has an irregular simple present, we will use the same irregular form when conjugating it as a reflexive/reciprocal verb. Remember that, of course, not all verbs have a corresponding reflexive/reciprocal form.

A few useful bits of information on some of the verbs conjugated in the table above. Let's start with **chiamarsi**. You definitely need to learn this verb by heart, because the first thing you are going to be asked, when talking to someone new in Italian, is **Come ti chiami?** It literally means *How do you call yourself?* but it really corresponds to the standard question *What is your name?*

You need the reflexive verb to ask and answer that question. To introduce yourself, you will have to say **Mi chiamo...**, which would be literally translated as *I call myself,* so *My name is...*

As for **decidersi**, you can see that the infinitive is followed by the preposition **a.** This is because, just like in English, that verb needs to be followed by that specific preposition. For example, you would say **Mi sono deciso a studiare all'estero**, *I have decided to study abroad.*

Even though the three conjugated verbs above are reflexive ones, the same applies to reciprocal verbs.

Examples: Ci baciamo ogni giorno, *We kiss each other every day;* **Si scambiano molte informazioni utili**, *They exchange a lot of useful information*, etc.

That is everything you need to know about reflexive and reciprocal verbs! At the end of this book, you will find a useful list of the most common reflexive and reciprocal verbs. Do not hesitate to take a look at them, and try to learn them little by little!

1. **Unisci l'immagine al verbo riflessivo o reciproco corrispondente.** *Link the image with the corresponding reflexive or reciprocal verb. Do not forget to check the verb lists at the end of the book.*

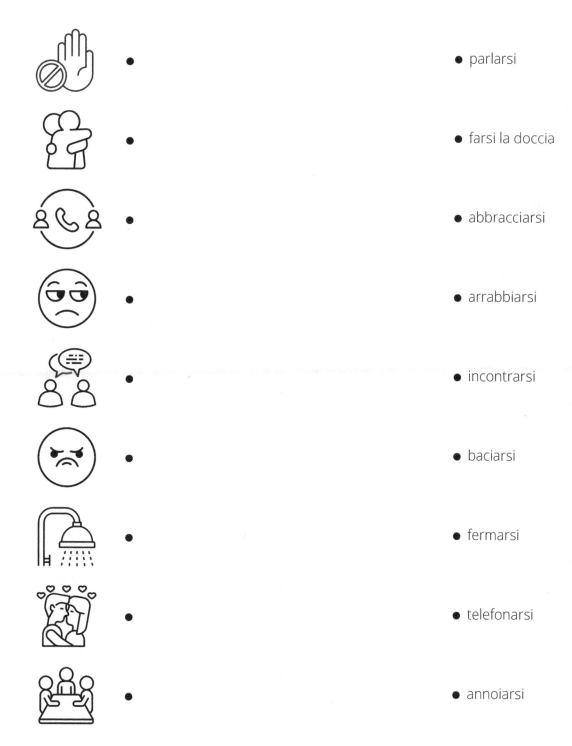

- parlarsi

- farsi la doccia

- abbracciarsi

- arrabbiarsi

- incontrarsi

- baciarsi

- fermarsi

- telefonarsi

- annoiarsi

2. Parla della tua routine mattutina. *Write about your morning routine using "ordinary" verbs, and reflexive and reciprocal ones. We have added part of the first sentence already.*

La mattina _____ alle _____ e _____

alle _____

_____

_____

_____

Translation

In the morning, I wake up at _____ and I get up at _____.

CHAPTER 3
SIMPLE PAST

Well, now that you've mastered verb conjugation in the simple present, it is time to learn how to talk in the *past tense*!

One of the things you should know is that, in Italian, there are two main tenses to talk about past actions/events — the **passato prossimo,** and the **imperfetto.** In this chapter, we are going to focus on the first one, and we will dedicate the next chapter to the other.

As we are going to introduce the so-called imperfect tense in the next chapter, now we will tell you that the **passato prossimo** must be used when talking about a past action/event that occurred at a precise moment in the past.

Good news. You are already familiar with this tense, but you do not know it yet. Well, to be honest, it may be a little confusing at first, but the structure of the passato prossimo is the same as the *present perfect* in English. **Examples with the present perfect:** *I have studied, She has been, They have seen,* etc.

As you can see, in order to form the present perfect, you need subject pronoun, auxiliary verb, and past participle of the main verb of the sentence. The passato prossimo shares the same construction. **Più o meno,** *more or less.*

First difference: as we have already said many times, subject pronouns are not really used in Italian, so there is no need to use them when talking in the past tense either.

Now, let's talk a bit about the auxiliary verb. In English, to form the present perfect, we only use the verb *to have*. Well, in Italian, the auxiliary verb can be *to be* OR *to have* – **essere o avere**. How can you know when you need to use one or the other?

Rest assured. Most of the Italian verbs require *to have* as the auxiliary. Take a look at the list below to find out which verbs require *to be:*

- Verbs expressing a movement, like **andare** *to go,* **venire** *to come,* **partire** *to leave,* etc.

- Verbs indicating a state of immobility, like **stare** *to stay,* **rimanere** *to remain,* **essere** *to be,* etc.

- Verbs indicating a change of state, like **diventare** *to become*, **cambiare** *to change*, **nascere** *to be born*, **morire** *to die*, etc.

- Reflexive and reciprocal verbs (see previous chapter and corresponding lists at the end of the book).

Of course, if you are not confident on how to conjugate the two auxiliary verbs, please take your time to review them before moving forward.

Now that we have the auxiliary, what is the third element left to add? The *past participle*. Just like in English, in Italian there are regular and irregular past participles. However, the irregular ones are *waaay* fewer than the English ones. Trust us when we tell you that the endless list of irregular English verbs is a real nightmare for Italian students.

As for the regular past participles, we will have to consider the usual three groups of verbs:

- The **-are** verbs have a past participle ending with **-ato**.

  Examples: parlare – parlato, *to speak – spoken*; **amare – amato**, *to love – loved*; **mangiare – mangiato**, *to eat – eaten*, **etc.**

- The **-ere** verbs have a past participle ending with **-uto**.

  Examples: credere – creduto, *to believe – believed*; **vendere – venduto**, *to sell – sold*; **cadere – caduto**, *to fall – fallen*, **etc.**

- The **-ire** verbs have a past participle ending with **-ito**.

  Examples: sentire – sentito, *to feel/hear – felt/heard*; **pulire – pulito**, *to clean – cleaned*; **guarire – guarito**, *to heal – healed*, **etc.**

In short, to form a past participle in Italian, you need to take the verb root and add the corresponding ending. As you may have noticed already, many irregular past participles in English are regular ones in Italian.

In order to help you recognize them, we added a list of the main verbs with an irregular past participle at the end of the book. Feel free to take a look every time you have doubts about a verb. **Non si sa mai!** *You never know!*

Now that you know which auxiliary verb you should use, and how to form a past participle, the next step is putting these elements together to conjugate your first verbs in the past tense!

Take a look at the table below. You will find the conjugation of three verbs in the past tense, one for each group.

	ANDARE *to go*	CREDERE *to believe*	CAPIRE *to understand*
io	sono andato/a	ho creduto	ho capito
tu	sei andato/a	hai creduto	hai capito
lui/lei/Lei	è andato/a	ha creduto	ha capito
noi	siamo andati/e	abbiamo creduto	abbiamo capito
voi	siete andati/e	avete creduto	avete capito
loro	sono andati/e	hanno creduto	hanno capito

In case you started panicking when you saw the conjugation of the first verb, **andare**, we can tell you that it is not as dramatic as it may seem. As you can see, that verb is the only one requiring *to be* as the auxiliary in the table above, as it is a verb of movement (see list above).

Well, whenever you use that auxiliary, you will have to adapt the past participle as well, meaning that you must choose its form — *masculine or feminine, singular or plural*. The signature endings are the same ones you learned when studying the adjectives, for example. The ending **-o** is masculine singular, **-a** feminine singular, **-i** masculine plural, **-e** feminine plural.

Using *to have* as the auxiliary is even easier. As you can see, the past participle never changes. It remains the same throughout the verb conjugation. No need to adapt it, no need to think about masculine, feminine, singular, plural, etc. The only thing you need to do is conjugate the auxiliary itself, obviously.

What happens when we want to conjugate a reflexive or a reciprocal verb in the past tense?

Honestly, not much. As we have already mentioned before, reflexive and reciprocal verbs need *to be* as the auxiliary. Whenever you need to use that auxiliary, you already know that you will have to choose the right form of the past participle. Also, do not forget that these are reflexive/reciprocal verbs. What else do you need, then? The reflexive pronouns, of course!

	VESTIRSI *to get dressed*	**PENTIRSI** *to regret*
io	mi sono vestito/a	mi sono pentito/a
tu	ti sei vestito/a	ti sei pentito/a
lui/lei/Lei	si è vestito/a	si è pentito/a
noi	ci siamo vestiti/e	ci siamo pentiti/e
voi	vi siete vestiti/e	vi siete pentiti/e
loro	si sono vestiti/e	si sono pentiti/e

See? There is not much to say. Whenever you are conjugating a reflexive or a reciprocal verb, do not forget to add the reflexive pronoun, use the auxiliary *to be*, and adapt the past participle accordingly.

One last thing. If you want to form a negative sentence, **non** goes before the reflexive pronoun.

Example: Non ci siamo preparate a casa sua, *We did not get ready at her place.*

This is all you need to know about the Italian **passato prossimo**. Let's finish this chapter with a few useful words and sentences.

ieri   *yesterday*

l'altroieri   *the day before yesterday*

una settimana/un mese/un anno fa   *a week/a month/a year ago*

la settimana scorsa/il mese scorso/l'anno scorso   *last week/month/year*

These expressions can go either at the beginning of a sentence, or at the end. In most cases, there will be no difference.

Examples:

- **Mia madre è partita per la Spagna l'anno scorso. Ci è andata con un'amica.**

  Last year, my mother left for Spain. She went there with a friend.

  Please note that the verb **partire** requires *to be* as the auxiliary because it is a verb of movement. Also, as the subject is a woman, we have to use the feminine singular form of the auxiliary. Another important note is about **"ci"**. This short word helps you avoid repeating previously mentioned words. **Ci è andata l'anno scorso = È andata in Spagna l'anno scorso.**

- **Ieri hanno avuto molte riunioni di lavoro.**

  Yesterday they had many business meetings.

  Even though the verb *to have* is very irregular when conjugated in the present tense, its past participle could not be more regular — **avere-avuto.**

- **Si sono trasferiti all'estero un mese fa.**

  They moved abroad a month ago.

  Please note that the English verb *to move* is a reflexive one in Italian — **trasferirsi —** and, as such, it requires the corresponding reflexive pronoun and *to be* as the auxiliary.

📝 EXERCISES III

1. Essere o avere? *Take a look at the verbs below, and mark whether they need the auxiliary* **to have** *(A) or* **to be** *(E).*

- prendere _____ *to take*

- venire _____ *to come*

- svegliarsi _____ *to wake up*

- cantare _____ *to sing*

- vedere _____ *to see*

- stare _____ *to stay*

- avvicinarsi _____ *to get closer*

- aprire _____ *to open*

2. E il participio passato? *Write the past participle of the verbs from the exercise above. Please note that there may be a few irregular ones!*

- prendere _____

- venire _____

- svegliarsi _____

- cantare _____

- vedere _____

- stare _____

- avvicinarsi _____

- aprire _____

3. Ascolta l'audio. *Listen to the audio file and add the missing verbs in the past tense.*

Dieci anni fa, _____ per la Germania per fare un semestre all'estero. _____

un'esperienza incredibile. Non solo _____ un'altra università e _____

un'altra lingua, ma _____ persone di tutto il mondo, che poi _____ miei

amici. _____ delle città magnifiche e non _____ per niente della mia scelta!

Translation

Ten years ago, I left for Germany to do a semester abroad. It has been a wonderful experience. I not only explored another university and learned a new language, but I also met people from all over the world, who then became my friends. I visited some beautiful cities, and I did not regret my choice at all!

CHAPTER 4
IMPERFECT TENSE

We know that you are probably asking yourself *Do I really need to know two past tenses in Italian?*

Unfortunately, the answer is yes. If you want to be fluent in Italian, you must learn both the **passato prossimo** and the **imperfetto —** the imperfect tense.

Good news, though. Everyone *LOVES* the imperfect tense, as it is probably the most regular one among all Italian tenses, as you are about to find out yourself.

In English, you would translate both these tenses with the simple past or the present perfect. But now a couple of questions naturally arise. What is the difference between them? When should I use one and when the other?

This "problem" may be a little tricky. If you remember, we have already said that the Italian simple past is used to describe actions or events that occurred in the past, at a precise moment in time. Well, to put it in a simple way, the imperfect tense is used when it comes to actions/events that had no specific duration in the past.

More specifically, we need the imperfect tense for:

- Habits, or to discuss something that happened regularly in the past. It is very common to use the imperfect tense when you talk about your childhood.

  Example: Andavo a scuola tutti i giorni. *I went to school every day.*

- After **mentre**, which corresponds to the English *while*. Please note that, in this instance, you generally use the imperfect tense in the sentence introduced by **mentre**, while the main sentence usually requires the **passato prossimo.**

  Example: Mentre studiavo, mi sono distratta. *I got distracted while I was studying.*

- Talking about emotions or feelings in the past.

  Example: Ieri era un po' triste. *Yesterday he/she was a bit sad.*

- Describing a dream/story.

  Example: Ero nella giungla, e una tigre mi inseguiva. *I was in the jungle and a tiger was chasing me.*

We know that, especially at the beginning, it may be hard for you to know when you must use the simple past and when to use the imperfect tense. However, it will get easier with practice. This is the reason why we always recommend using as many resources as possible, so that you can train your ear and get used to this tense.

Now, moving on to the fun stuff. The verb conjugation in the imperfect tense.

First, good news: no auxiliary needed. Just like the present tense, you will start your sentence with the conjugated verb directly.

This is how you form the imperfect tense for the three groups of Italian verbs:

- **-are** verbs: verb root + **AV** + endings

- **-ere** verbs: verb root + **EV** + endings

- **-ire** verbs: verb root + **IV** + endings

It seems quite easy, doesn't it? It is. Take a look at the table below to see the conjugation of three Italian verbs in the imperfect tense.

	SALTARE *to jump*	**VEDERE** *to see*	**STARNUTIRE** *to sneeze*
io	salt-av-o	ved-ev-o	starnut-iv-o
tu	saltavi	vedevi	starnutivi
lui/lei/Lei	saltava	vedeva	starnutiva
noi	saltavamo	vedevamo	starnutivamo
voi	saltavate	vedevate	starnutivate
loro	saltavano	vedevano	starnutivano

We broke down the first conjugated verbs so that you could see the different sections we mentioned above.

Do you notice something when you look at the verb endings? Yes, they are the same for the three groups of verbs! Heaven, isn't it? We would say so.

Now you know why all students love this tense. Its structure is very easy and it repeats itself for all the verbs.

Well, if now we told you there are three main verbs with an irregular conjugation, would you be mad at us? We know, at the beginning of this chapter we told you that the conjugation in the imperfect tense is very regular, but *c'mon*, we are talking about just three irregular verbs out of hundreds of Italian verbs!

Without further ado, let's look at them.

Via il dente, via il dolore! *End the problem, end the pain!*

	ESSERE *to be*	**FARE** *to do/make*	**DIRE** *to say*
io	e-ro	fa-cevo	di-cevo
tu	eri	facevi	dicevi
lui/lei/Lei	era	faceva	diceva
noi	eravamo	facevamo	dicevamo
voi	eravate	facevate	dicevate
loro	erano	facevano	dicevano

As you can see, these verbs are considered irregular because they do not follow the (few) rules of the imperfect tense. For **essere**, we are not using its verb root to form the imperfect tense — which would be **ess-**. And not only that. We have the **-av-** block only for the plural subject pronouns. What can we say... the verb *to be* always wants to feel special.

As for **fare** and **dire**, these two verbs are *almost* regular ones. We say almost because their verb roots would be **f-** and **d-**, respectively. Just one letter. Before the **-EV-** or **-IV-** block, then, we needed to add a couple of extra letters — **ac** and **ic**, respectively.

Of course, there are other past tenses in Italian, but we will stop here because not only we do not want you to have a migraine, but also these two are the main ones you need to know to start talking in Italian right away.

 **EXERCISES IV**

1. **Coniuga i verbi.** *Conjugate the verbs in the table below in the imperfect tense.*

	PAGARE *to pay*	**VENDERE** *to sell*	**COSTRUIRE** *to build*
io			
tu			
lui/lei/Lei			
noi			
voi			
loro			

2. **Imperfetto o passato prossimo?** *Take a look at the sentences below, and add the missing verb. You will have to conjugate it either in the simple past or in the imperfect tense. Please note that there may be some irregular verbs.*

• Ieri _____ una nuova bicicletta. (comprare, io)

Yesterday I bought a new bike.

• I cugini _____ sempre insieme. (giocare, loro)

The cousins always played together.

• _____ mai _____ a Madrid? (essere, tu)

Have you ever been to Madrid?

• _____ che quest'anno si licenzieranno. (noi, scoprire)

We found out that this year they will quit.

• Da piccolo _____ tantissimi amici a scuola. (avere, lui)

When he was a child, he had many friends in school.

- Mentre _____, _____ una chiamata. (mangiare-ricevere, noi).

  We received a call while we were eating.

3. **Cos'hai sognato?** *Describe a dream you had. Feel free to use the dictionary for help.*

_____

_____

_____

_____

_____

_____

EXTRA
TONGUE TWISTERS!

Ready to have a little bit of fun with the Italian language and challenge yourself with some new tongue twisters? Be ready, because the following ones will be as hard as the ones you read at the end of the previous unit.

Buona fortuna! *Good luck!*

· **Dietro il palazzo c'è un povero cane pazzo, date un pezzo di pane al povero pazzo cane.**

Yeah, another Italian tongue twister involving (sad) animals. The translation of this one is *Behind the building there is a poor crazy dog, give the poor crazy dog a piece of bread*. The hard part here is the repetition of similar words like **palazzo, pazzo, pezzo.** You will see that it is quite difficult to pronounce them correctly one after the other.

Pronunciation: d*ee-eh-troh eel pah-lah-dzoh chèh oon poh-veh-roh kah-neh pah-dzoh, dah-teh oon peh-dzoh dee pah-neh ahl poh-veh-roh pah-dzoh kah-neh.*

- **Sul tagliere gli agli taglia, non tagliare la tovaglia; la tovaglia non è aglio, se la tagli fai uno sbaglio.**

This is a fun one playing with one of the most difficult sounds in Italian — **gl.** The translation of this tongue twister is *Cut the garlic on the cutting board, do not cut the tablecloth; the tablecloth is not garlic, if you cut it you make a mistake.* Well, it does not make much sense — as with most of these tongue twisters — but it is very hard not to mispronounce those words!

Pronunciation: *sool tah-lleh-reh llee ah-llee tah-lleah, nohn tah-lleah-reh lah toh-vah-lleah; lah toh-vah-lleeah nohn èh ah-lleoh, she lah tah-llee fah-e oo-noh sbah-lleoh.*

UNIT 4

BUILDING YOUR FIRST SENTENCES

CHAPTER 1

EVERYDAY LIFE

After the *huuuge* effort of learning articles, prepositions, verb tenses... you deserve to relax a little bit. And while learning a new language, there is no better way to relax than focusing on vocabulary only.

This is exactly what we will do in this chapter. Of course, it is important to know how to conjugate verbs and how to use the possessive adjectives and all the other fun things, but you should learn some vocabulary as well!

Are you going to travel or work in Italy? Well, you need to learn the days of the week and the months — **i giorni della settimana e i mesi**. If you do not know them, how are you going to book a table at a restaurant? Or a hotel room?

Please note that, if you are going to visit/live in one of the major Italian cities, most people — especially the young — will speak at least a little bit of English. However, if you are planning on visiting those charming little villages, do not take for granted that people will speak English. This is the reason why it is always better to learn a few useful words.

Let's start with the days of the week:

lunedì	*Monday*
martedì	*Tuesday*
mercoledì	*Wednesday*
giovedì	*Thursday*
venerdì	*Friday*
sabato	*Saturday*
domenica	*Sunday*

A few things to notice about the days of the week:

- The Italian ones do not require a capital letter as they do in English. They will have a capital letter only when they are the first word of a sentence.

- Most of them — from Monday to Friday — have that weird accent on the last *i*. Why, though? Well, because in old Italian, the word **dì** meant *day*.

- All days of the week are masculine, except for Sunday.

- The days of the week, in most cases, do not need a preposition like in English. You would say **lunedì vado al lavoro** — *On Monday I go to work.*

Is there a reason behind the Italian names of the days of the week? Yes, there is!

Most of them owe their names to the planets. Let's discover the origin of their names along with their English translation:

GIORNO DELLA SETTIMANA *day of the week*	NOME ORIGINALE *original name*	TRADUZIONE *translation*
lunedì	lunae dies (Latin)	*the day of the Moon*
martedì	martis dies (Latin)	*the day of Mars*
mercoledì	mercuri dies (Latin)	*the day of Mercury*
giovedì	iovis dies (Latin)	*the day of Jupiter*
venerdì	veneris dies (Latin)	*the day of Venus*
sabato	shabbat (Hebrew)	*rest day*
domenica	dominica (Latin)	*the day of God*

A couple of **fun facts**. As you can see, **sabato** is different from the other days. Originally, it was **Saturni dies**, *the day of Saturn.* Does the Latin word remind you something? Yes, *Saturday!*

The same applies to *Sunday*. The original name of this day, in Latin, was **Solis dies**, *the day of the Sun.* It is not a coincidence that we have the same origin also in other languages, like German — where Sunday is **Sonntag**.

Let's move forward and learn the months now — **i mesi**.

gennaio	*January*	**luglio**	*July*
febbraio	*February*	**agosto**	*August*
marzo	*March*	**settembre**	*September*
aprile	*April*	**ottobre**	*October*
maggio	*May*	**novembre**	*November*
giugno	*June*	**dicembre**	*December*

As you can see, the names of the months in Italian are not that different from the English ones, especially from September onwards.

We do not want to bore you with the etymology of each month, but allow us to explain why *August* is called this way. Well, this month originally had a different name, which was then changed in honor of **Augustus**, the first emperor of the Roman Empire.

Also, once again, Italian months do not require a capital letter, but they need the preposition **a**. **Example: A gennaio ricomincia la scuola**. *In January, school starts again.*

When talking about dates, you need to know how to translate *When* — **quando. Example: Quando vai in vacanza? A luglio.** *When are you going on holiday? In July.*

Finally, keep in mind that the Italian date format is the following: **DD/MM/YY — giorno/mese/anno**. For example, if you see 06/07/2022, that means July 6th, 2022. **Example: Che giorno è oggi? Il tre settembre**. *What day is it? It is September 3rd.*

As we are discussing days, months and years, let's not forget the seasons — **le stagioni!**

autunno	*autumn*
inverno	*winter*
primavera	*spring*
estate	*summer*

When talking about the seasons, the preposition you must use is **in**.

Example: In inverno è sempre freddo. *In winter it is always cold.*

 FALSE FRIEND ALERT! The Italian adjective **caldo** does not mean *cold*, but quite the opposite! It means hot. The adjective for *cold* is **freddo**.

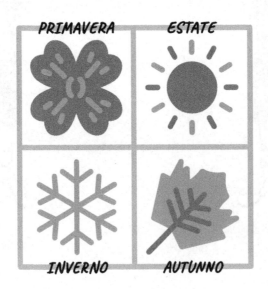

 **EXERCISES I**

1. **Scrivi la traduzione in inglese o in italiano.** *Fill in the table with the missing Italian or English translations of the days of the week and the months.*

ENG	ITA
Tuesday	
	domenica
March	
Wednesday	
	giugno
October	
	agosto
July	
	giovedì
Saturday	
January	

2. **Rispondi alle seguenti domande.** *Answer the following questions in Italian. Try to use as many words as possible.*

- **Quando è il tuo compleanno?**   *When is your birthday?*

  _____

- **Che giorno è oggi?**   *What day is it?*

  _____

- **Qual è il tuo mese preferito?**   *What is your favorite month?*

  _____

- **Qual è la tua stagione preferita?**   *What is your favorite season?*

  _____

CHAPTER 2
TELLING THE TIME

Now that you know how to say the date, and all the Italian names for the days and months, it is time to talk about *time*.

First of all, is it true that Italians are always late? It depends. Some people are always late; others are as punctual as the Germans (speaking of stereotypes...). One thing is sure, though. When Italians arrive 5–10 minutes late, most likely they don't think they are late. Being 5–10 mins late is not considered being that late, unless it's about an important work work appointment or something like that.

Learning how to tell the time is very important. Yes, nowadays we all have smartphones that tell us the time, but you need to understand when someone is telling you a specific time, and you have to know how to tell the time yourself. For example, if you want to book a table at a restaurant, or if you are on the phone trying to get an appointment with your Italian doctor.

The first question you should learn, then, is **Che ore sono?** *What time is it?*

As you may have noticed already, we are asking that question using the plural form — **che ore sono** — as the hours are always plural by definition (after all, they are plural numbers!). Well, there is actually just one exception. More about it in a bit.

Another thing you should know, before moving forward, is that Italians use the **24-hour** format, but they would use it in more formal situations. More commonly, they would use the 12-hour format, but without a.m. or p.m. In fact, in general, it is usually clear whether you are talking about a specific time in the morning or in the afternoon/evening. They may use the 24-hour format, for example, when booking appointments.

For example, if you say **Pranzo all'una** — *I have lunch at 1* — it is not necessary to say 13 or p.m., as people would not have lunch at 1 a.m. On the other hand, if someone says **Inizio il lavoro alle otto** — *I start working at eight* — in this instance, they will probably specify if they mean morning or evening by saying *eight* or *twenty*.

24-hour time		
0 1 2 3 4 5 6 7 8 9 10 11 12 13 14 15 16 17 18 19 20 21 22 23		
a.m.		p.m.
12 1 2 3 4 5 6 7 8 9 10 11 12 1 2 3 4 5 6 7 8 9 10 11		
12-hour time		

Moving forward, now that you know how to ask what time it is, let's find out how to answer that question! In the table below, you will find a few options.

| ORA
hour	ITA	ENG
8:00	sono le otto (in punto)	*it is eight o' clock*
1:00	è l'una (in punto)	*it is one o' clock*
8:15	sono le otto e un quarto / e quindici	*it is a quarter past eight / eight fifteen*
8:20	sono le otto e venti	*it is twenty past eight*
8:30	sono le otto e mezzo / e trenta	*it is half past eight / eight thirty*
8:45	sono le nove meno un quarto / le otto e quarantacinque	*it is a quarter to nine / eight forty-five*
8:55	sono le nove meno cinque / le otto e cinquantacinque	*it is five to nine / eight fifty-five*
12:00	sono le dodici / è mezzogiorno	*it is twelve o' clock / midday*
00:00	è mezzanotte	*it is midnight*

We know that it may seem overwhelming at first, but you will soon find out that it is not that different from what we say in English. A few things to highlight:

- Yeah... unfortunately, when you tell the time, every hour needs its *definite article*. However, as already anticipated, all hours are plural and feminine, meaning that their article will always be **le.** The only exception is **1,** as it is a singular number. This is why the verb *to be* is in its singular form, and its definite article is **l'** — which is the singular definite article we use for nouns beginning with a vowel.

- For the first two examples, you can see that we added that **in punto** in brackets. It means *on the dot,* and you can either say it or not. It is up to you.

- In Italian, they do not say *past*. For example, they say *It is ten* and *five* — 10:05. As for *to,* it is replaced by **meno** — *minus*. They say *It is eleven* minus *ten* — 10:50. It makes sense, doesn't it?

- In some instances, you have two options, just like in English. Saying *half past / a quarter past / a quarter to* is a bit more informal. In general, if you go for the option with the minutes — as it is more formal — you will use the 24-hour format as well.

  Example: sono le diciassette e trenta OR **sono le cinque e mezzo.**

- *Midnight* and *midday* are singular words, so they require the verb *to be* in its singular form. Also, they do not need a definite article.

  Example: È mezzanotte.

What happens when someone asks you a question like *What time is the football match*, for example? Well, for starters, the translation of that kind of question is **A che ora...?**

When you answer, in English, you would use *at* before the time. In Italian, you need a preposition too, and that preposition is **a**.

Wait a minute... if you remember, we have just said that, in Italian, every hour needs its definite article. And what happens if we combine a preposition + a definite article? Yes... an articulated preposition, *again*. This is the reason why we told you that it is very important to learn them! They are *E-V-E-R-Y-W-H-E-R-E*.

As only two definite articles are involved in telling the time — **le** and **l'** — there are only two options for the articulated prepositions — **alle** and **all'**, respectively.

Examples:

Vado dal dentista alle cinque.   *I go to the dentist at five.*

Mi hanno invitato a pranzo all'una.   *They invited me for lunch at one.*

To finish this chapter, we would like to add just a few more useful words regarding the parts of the day, and of course... the meals!

mattino	*morning*
colazione	*breakfast*
fare colazione	*to have breakfast*
pomeriggio	*afternoon*
pranzo	*lunch*
pranzare	*to have lunch*
merenda	*afternoon snack*
sera	*evening*
cena	*dinner*
cenare	*to have dinner*
spuntino di mezzanotte	*midnight snack*

This is all you need to know! Of course, you will make mistakes. And it is perfectly normal. As well as doing our exercises in the following section, we also recommend doing a very simple yet effective exercise that you should do every day, wherever you are. It will take only a few seconds of your time.

Every once in a while, try to look at your watch/phone, and tell the time in Italian. You will see that you will start telling the time more fluently and without mistakes in just a short amount of time. **Provare per credere!** *Seeing is believing!*

📝 EXERCISES II

1. **Scrivi l'ora corrispondente.** *Write the time in Italian. If there is more than just one option, please write them both.*

   - 12:00 _____
   - 13:15 _____
   - 4:30 _____
   - 18:25 _____
   - 22:45 _____
   - 00:00 _____
   - 7:55 _____
   - 19:00 _____

2. **Rispondi alle seguenti domande.** *Answer the following questions.*

   - **A che ora ti svegli la mattina?**   *What time do you wake up in the morning?*

   _____

   - **Che ore sono adesso?**   *What time is it now?*

   _____

   - **A che ora ceni di solito?**   *What time do you usually have dinner?*

   _____

   - **A che ora inizi a lavorare?**   *What time do you start working?*

   _____

   - **A che ora c'è il tramonto?**   *What time is the sunset?*

   _____

CHAPTER 3
THE VERB TO LIKE

A whole chapter on the verb *to like?* Is it really needed?

Well, yes, it is. The verb *to like* in Italian — **piacere,** a verb of the **-ere** group **—** is not complicated, nor impossible to learn. It is just a little bit... different. You just need to learn how to conjugate it. That's it.

And of course, you *must* learn how to conjugate it. How many times a day do we use this verb? It becomes even more important when you are traveling or spending some time abroad.

In English, the verb *to like* is just like the other regular verbs. *I like writing books on Italian grammar,* for example. In Italian, the structure of this verb is slightly different. We would say *Writing books on Italian grammar is pleasing to me.* Do not look at the structure of the sentence itself, but just the verb.

In Italian, *to me* is needed, and we place it at the beginning of the sentence, as if it were *"To me is pleasing writing books on Italian grammar".* This is how a sentence with the verb **piacere** would look, as much as it may seem weird in English.

In short, we need the indirect object pronoun at the beginning of the sentence... *yes, them, again!* In case you have forgotten them — or were hoping to forget them — we invite you to revise the indirect object pronouns in our Unit 2, Chapter 5.

Also, as we are using an indirect object pronoun, we are never going to use the subject pronoun as well. Think about it. You would never say *I to me.*

Now let's take a look at the conjugation of this verb:

MI PIACE / PIACCIONO	I like
TI PIACE / PIACCIONO	you like
GLI / LE PIACE / PIACCIONO	he/she/it likes
CI PIACE / PIACCIONO	we like
VI PIACE / PIACCIONO	you like
A LORO PIACE / PIACCIONO	they like

Why two options? It is a very easy rule to understand, and it is even easier to apply. When someone likes one thing only, they will use **piace** — singular. If they like two or more things — or a plural noun — then they will use **piacciono** — plural. If you like doing something — and one <u>or more</u> verbs follow the verb *to like* — you will have to use **piace**.

Examples:

Mi piace la lingua italiana.   *I like the Italian language.*

Ti piacciono le preposizioni articolate.   *You like the articulated prepositions.*

A loro piace studiare l'Italiano.   *They like studying Italian.*

If you want to say that you do not like something, you will just have to add a **non** in front of the indirect object pronoun.

Examples:

Non ci piace il temporale.   *We do not like the storm.*

Non ci piacciono le ciliegie.   *We do not like cherries. (Who does not like them, though?)*

As for the third person singular, you can see that we have two options for the indirect object pronoun. You will have to use **gli** if the person liking something is male, and **le** if that person is female.

When you are using the simple past — the **passato prossimo** in Italian — the verb piacere requires *to be* as the auxiliary.

Example: Mi è piaciuta l'ultima vacanza.   *I liked the last holiday.*

Before finishing this chapter, let's add a few useful words/expressions that may come in handy, as we often use the verb *to like* when talking about food.

sono vegetariano/a	*I am vegetarian*
sono vegano/a	*I am vegan*
sono allergico/a a...	*I am allergic to...*
sono intollerante a...	*I am intolerant to...*
sono celiaco/a	*I am celiac*
non posso mangiare...	*I cannot eat...*
sono astemio/a	*I don't drink*
sono a dieta	*I am on a diet*

Regarding the last sentence above, we would not recommend going to Italy if you are on a diet. Unless you have very strong willpower...

See? It was not that hard. Now it is time to start practicing. **Andiamo!** *Let's go!*

✍️ EXERCISES III

1. Scrivi cosa ti piace e cosa non ti piace. *Write a few sentences in Italian about what you like and do not like.*

Mi piace / piacciono

_____

_____

_____

Non mi piace / piacciono

_____

_____

_____

🎧 **2. Ascolta l'audio.** *Listen to the audio file and add the missing words.*

Una delle cose che _____ di più è suonare il sax. _____ la musica

jazz e _____ blues. Abbiamo _____ e _____

ogni settimana per suonare _____ La prossima settimana abbiamo il nostro primo

_____! Siamo molto _____.

Translation

One of the things we like the most is playing the sax. We love jazz music and blues singers. We have a band and we meet every week to play together. Next week we have our first concert! We are very excited.

CHAPTER 4
TALKING ABOUT THE FUTURE

You know how to talk in the present tense, you know how to talk about the past. Let's not forget your future plans, though!

Maybe this is something we should not tell you, but as we are always *very* honest with our students... When you want to discuss something that will happen in the future, in Italian you can often use the present tense, even though it would not be very correct in terms of grammar. What we are suggesting is: use the present tense only as **ultima spiaggia —** literally *as a last beach*, meaning as a last resort.

In fact, knowing how to conjugate a verb in the future tense is always helpful. Also, **il futuro semplice** — *Future I* — is not hard at all, so it will not require a huge effort on your part. And if you think about it, you are here, reading this book, because you *want* to challenge yourself, right?

Once again, the Italian language will surprise you. You know that Italian students *HATE* the future in English? Why? Because there are three types of future! They get too used to conjugating verbs in English in an easy way. Not that the future tenses in English are *that* difficult, but still, students have to think about which one to use: *simple present*, *to be going to*, *will*...

⚠️ **GOOD NEWS:**

In Italian, there is just one option for the future. You would use the **futuro semplice** and that's it.

Let's keep on talking about differences. First of all, in Italian, you do not need an auxiliary verb like in English. The conjugated verb in the future tense is made of the verb root and the specific endings of this tense. In the table below, you will see three conjugated verbs, one for each Italian verb group, and then we will explain everything you need to know about this tense.

	GUIDARE *to drive*	SCEGLIERE *to choose*	AGIRE *to take action*
io	guid-erò	scegli-erò	ag-irò
tu	guiderai	sceglierai	agirai
lui/lei/Lei	guiderà	sceglierà	agirà
noi	guideremo	sceglieremo	agiremo
voi	guiderete	sceglierete	agirete
loro	guideranno	sceglieranno	agiranno

As you can see, the verbs belonging to the **-are** and **-ere** groups share the same endings. The verb ending with **-ire** has only the *e* of the verb ending replaced with an *i*. Everything else is the same for the three groups. Do not forget the accent when you conjugate the verb for the subject pronouns *I* and *he/she*/it. Well, the future tense in Italian is not that hard, is it?

Examples:

Studieremo Letteratura all'università.   *We will study literature at the university.*

Studieremo is the verb **studiare** conjugated in the future tense according to the subject pronoun **noi**.

Prenderà la patente a 18 anni.   *He/She will get his/her driver's license at 18.*

Prenderà is the verb **prendere** conjugated in the future tense. Also, please note that in Europe teens cannot get their driver's license before turning 18. If you want to drive a small scooter — **un motorino,** like a *Vespa* — you can get a specific license at 14 years old, though.

Mamma, pulirò la camera domani.   *Mom, I will clean my room tomorrow.*

Pulirò is the verb **pulire** conjugated in the future tense. Please note that **domani** could be placed right after the comma, and the meaning of the sentence would remain the same.

Now that you know how to conjugate regular verbs in the future tense, we should get to the "hard" part and show you the conjugation in the future tense of two of the most used verbs, and also the most irregular ones — **essere e avere**, *to be* and *to have*.

	ESSERE *to be*	**AVERE** *to have*
io	sarò	avrò
tu	sarai	avrai
lui/lei/Lei	sarà	avrà
noi	saremo	avremo
voi	sarete	avrete
loro	saranno	avranno

As you can see, the verb *to be* does not use its verb root — which would be **ess-**. *To have*, on the other hand, doesn't have the signature *e* of the verb ending in the future tense — as a reminder, it should have been **av-erò**. Do you know that there are other verbs behaving just like **avere**? Take a look at the verbs in the table below:

INFINITO *infinitive*	**FUTURO** *future tense*
andare to go	**and-rò, andrai, andrà...** *I will go, you will go, etc.*
cadere to fall	**cad-rò, cadrai, cadrà...** *I will fall, etc.*
dovere must / have to	**dov-rò, dovrai, dovrà...** *I will have to, etc.*
potere can / to be able to	**pot-rò, potrai, potrà...** *I will be able to, etc.*
sapere to know	**sap-rò, saprai, saprà...** *I will know, etc.*
vedere to see	**ved-rò, vedrai, vedrà...** *I will see, etc.*
vivere to live	**viv-rò, vivrai, vivrà...** *I will live, etc.*

Anything else? Well, just a couple of things. There is another group of irregular verbs whose infinitive ends with **-ciare** and **-giare**. Do not worry. The only thing you will have to do when conjugating these verbs in the future tense is delete the *i* in the verb root. For example, you will say **Comincerò a fare i bagagli** — *I will start packing* — and not **comincierò.**

Here's a very short list of the most common verbs ending with **-ciare**:

baciare (bacerò)	*to kiss*
bilanciare (bilancerò)	*to balance*
cominciare (comincerò)	*to start/begin*
lasciare (lascerò)	*to leave*
rinfacciare (rinfaccerò)	*to hold against somebody*
verniciare (vernicerò)	*to paint (walls, for example, but not a canvas)*

And the most common **-giare** verbs:

danneggiare (danneggerò)	*to damage*
mangiare (mangerò)	*to eat*
noleggiare (noleggerò)	*to rent (a car, for example, but not an apartment)*
parcheggiare (parcheggerò)	*to park*
sfoggiare (sfoggerò)	*to show off*
viaggiare (viaggerò)	*to travel*

Very last thing, we promise you. All verbs ending with **-care** and **-gare** require an additional *h* before the endings of the future to keep the hard sound of the infinitive (we already discussed this point when explaining the simple present in Italian, do you remember?). It means that you will say **Pagherò il conto** — *I will pay the* bill — and not **pagerò.**

A few common verbs ending with **-care**:

cercare (cercherò)	*to look for / search*
cliccare (cliccherò)	*to click*

giocare (giocherò)	*to play (a game, but not an instrument)*
pescare (pescherò)	*to fish*
scroccare (scroccherò)	*to scrounge*
toccare (toccherò)	*to touch*

And here are a few **-gare** verbs as well:

allargare (allargherò)	*to widen*
allegare (allegherò)	*to attach (a file to an email, for example)*
negare (negherò)	*to deny*
obbligare (obbligherò)	*to force*
pagare (pagherò)	*to pay*
piegare (piegherò)	*to fold*

There is nothing else to say about the future tense in terms of grammar. Of course, we could talk about Future II — for example *I will have finished my studies* — but we chose to focus on the simple future in order to give you all the tools you need to start talking about future events without feeling overwhelmed.

Before moving on to the exercises, in the list below you will find some useful words/expressions related to the future:

domani	*tomorrow*
dopodomani	*the day after tomorrow*
tra un giorno / un mese	*in a day / a month*
l'anno prossimo	*next year*
la settimana prossima	*next week*

✏️ EXERCISES IV

1. **Coniuga i verbi al futuro semplice.** *Conjugate the verbs in the table below in the future tense.*

	CONTROLLARE *to check*	NEGARE *to deny*	SUGGERIRE *to suggest*
io			
tu			
lui/lei/Lei			
noi			
voi			
loro			

2. Rispondi alle domande usando il futuro. *Answer the following questions using the future tense. Do not hesitate to use the dictionary for help.*

- Che cosa farai domani? *What are you doing tomorrow?*

  _____

  _____

- Che programmi hai per il prossimo fine settimana? *What are your plans for next weekend?*

  _____

  _____

- Come ti vedi tra cinque anni? *Where do you see yourself in five years?*

  _____

  _____

EXTRA
TONGUE TWISTERS!

Our last section with Italian tongue twisters. We know, we know. It is sad. This is the reason why we saved the most difficult ones for last *evil laugh*.

Ready to challenge yourself one last time?

Trentatré trentini entrarono a Trento, tutti e trentatré trotterellando.

This is one of the hardest Italian tongue twisters because of the continuous repetition of the *tr* sound, which can be even more difficult to pronounce for English speakers. It means: *Thirty-three people from Trento entered Trento, all of them trotting along.* Why? We do not know.

Pronunciation: *trehn-tah-treh trehn-tee-nee ehn-trah-roh-noh ah trehn-toh, too-tee eh trehn-tah-treh troht-teh-rehl-lahn-doh.*

Apelle, figlio d'Apollo, fece una palla di pelle di pollo; tutti i pesci vennero a galla per vedere la palla di pelle di pollo, fatta da Apelle, figlio d'Apollo.

Whoa! Yes, this is a long one. As you can see, this tongue twister is all about the repetition of the letter *p* followed by different vowels. Its translation is: *Apelle, son of Apollo, made a ball of chicken skin (?!); all the fish came to the surface to see the ball of chicken skin made by Apelle, son of Apollo.*

Pronunciation: *ah-pehl-leh fee-lleoh dee ah-pohl-loh feh-che oona pahl-lah dee pehl-leh dee pohl-loh; too-tee ee peh-she vehn-neh-roh ah gahl-lah pehr veh-deh-reh lah pahl-lah dee pehl-leh dee pohl-loh, faht-tah dah ah-pehl-leh, fee-lleoh dee ah-pohl-loh.*

UNIT 5

EXTRA: HOW-TO GUIDE

CHAPTER 1
GOING SHOPPING AT THE SUPERMARKET

First of all, congratulations! You've almost reached the end of this book. And not only that: in this unit, you will not find anything grammar-related! Now we really want to focus on practical and useful vocabulary. For example, when you go to Italy, you will probably go shopping, or to the supermarket. And there are a few things you should know.

One of the things most people who have been to Italy tend to say is that Italians are well-dressed even when they go to the supermarket. Well... Italians think it is just normal. You will see people wearing a tracksuit, of course, but do not expect to see someone wearing their pajamas in a supermarket.

Here's a short list of useful supermarket-related vocabulary:

supermercato	*supermarket*	**banco forno**	*bakery*
fare la spesa	*grocery shopping*	**commesso**	*shop assistant*
reparto	*aisle*	**cassiere**	*cashier*
macelleria	*butcher shop*	**cassa**	*till*
pescheria	*fish shop*	**busta**	*shopping bag*
surgelati	*frozen food*	**carrello**	*cart*
frutta e verdure	*fruit and vegetables*	**uscita senza acquisti**	*exit without purchases*
prodotti per l'igiene	*personal care products*		

Of course, these are just some useful words. We could probably write a whole book on this topic, especially if we start discussing all the amazing food sold in Italian supermarkets.

Moving on to practical scenarios, you should always keep a 1€ coin in your wallet. *Why?* Because most Italian supermarkets have carts that are unlocked with a 1€ coin. Do not worry. The cart will not eat you precious coin. You will get it back as soon as you bring the cart back to where you took it from.

If you are going to buy a fresh product — whether it is meat, fish, bread, or a ready-made meal — you will probably have to take a ticket with a number and wait for your turn. As soon as your number appears on the screen, you are good to go. If you do not want to get into an argument with an angry customer, never forget to take your ticket, *NEVER!*

Please note that nowadays, in every big supermarket, you will find vegetarian and vegan options, along with food for people with celiac disease or for all those with special food requirements. In case of doubt, ask for those **reparti.** For example, you can ask **Mi scusi, mi sa dire dov'è il reparto di...?** *Excuse-me, could you tell me where the ..... aisle is?*

Then, when it is time to pay, you might have to ask the cashier for shopping bags. The question you should ask is **Posso avere una/due/tre busta/buste?** *Can I have one/two/three shopping bag(s)?*

When it comes to paying, you should tell the cashier how you want to pay: **in contanti** – *cash* — or **con la carta —** *by card.* Once they give you the receipt, you are free to go with your groceries.

Of course, as we are talking about shopping, we cannot help but mention the names of the different kinds of Italian shops. Take a look at the list below to find out their names in Italian:

negozio	*shop/store*
negozio di scarpe	*shoe store*
negozio di vestiti	*clothes store*
centro commerciale	*mall*

gioielleria	*jewelry store*
negozio per bambini	*kids' store*
bar	*café*
ristorante	*restaurant*
parrucchiere	*hairdresser's*
farmacia	*pharmacy*
edicola	*newsstand*
libreria	*bookstore*
ottico	*optician store*
fioraio	*florist*
panificio / forno	*bakery*
vivaio	*garden centre*
ferramenta	*hardware store*
profumeria	*beauty store*
tabaccheria	*tobacco store (selling cigarettes, but also stamps, etc.)*

If you are looking for one of these shops, you just need to ask **Dov'è / Dove sono...?** *Where is / Where are...?* Do not forget to add the corresponding definite article in front of the store, though.

Speaking of directions, you should also learn how to say *right* — **destra** — and *left* — **sinistra.** And here are other useful direction words:

davanti a	*in front of*
dietro a	*behind*
vicino a	*near*
accanto a	*next to*

Please note that, even though all Italian shops are required by law to accept card payments as of summer 2022, it is always best to have some cash with you. **Non si sa mai.** *You never know.*

Also, always make sure that the items you are interested in have a price tag. If they do not have one, you should ask the question **Quanto costa?** or **Quanto costano**? — respectively, *How much is it?* and *How much are they?*

A quick test to check whether you have studied or not: *How would you pronounce the word euro in Italian?*

It is read as *eh-oo-roh*. Do not forget that Italians read all the letters in a word. Also, the word *euro* is invariable, meaning that you will say **1 euro, 2 euro, 10,000 euro.**

When it comes to opening hours, it really depends on where you are. In big cities, some shops never close during the day, but others close at lunch time. When this happens, usually they close around 12:30 or 1 p.m. and re-open between 3 and 3:30 p.m.

It is also very unlikely to find shops that open at 8 a.m. — unless they are pharmacies, bakeries, and cafés. Most shops open around 9 a.m., or even 10 a.m. in some cities, and they usually close around 7–8 p.m.

✎ EXERCISES I

1. **Collega i negozi con la loro traduzione.** *Link the shops to their Italian translation.*

        ●   ● parrucchiere

        ●   ● macelleria

        ●   ● edicola

        ●   ● gioielleria

        ●   ● pescheria

        ●   ● negozio di scarpe

        ●   ● forno

2. Ascolta l'audio. *Listen to the audio file and add the missing words.*

Oggi io e le mie amiche siamo andate a _____! Avevo bisogno di

un paio nuovo di _____, quindi quella è stata la nostra prima tappa. Poi una mia

amica voleva comprare una rivista all' _____. Ho comprato anche il _____

per mia madre. Avevamo fame e per la merenda siamo andate al _____ vicino al

_____. È il migliore della _____.

CHAPTER 2
EATING

Well, if you are planning on going to Italy, you cannot skip this section. Eating is something we all do, but some countries, Italy in particular, have plenty of local traditions and habits. Italians are *veeery* strict when it comes to food. You may know this already if you have been to Italy before.

We have already mentioned the Italian names of meals in the chapter about the days of the week and the months, so now it is time to discuss them in detail.

- **Colazione** *Breakfast*   Anytime from 8:30 to 11:00 a.m.

The typical Italian breakfast would include a coffee — **un espresso,** of course! — or a **cappuccino** with a croissant. *Beware!* A cappuccino is supposed to be drunk for breakfast only. If you drink one after lunch or dinner, you give *tourist vibes* — and will probably get a funny look from the other Italian customers in the restaurant! But if you *really* want to, go ahead! Italians would understand and they *love* tourists, anyway.

If you want to have a very Italian breakfast, you should go to a local **bar**. Breakfasts are mainly sweet in Italy. You can find plain croissants, or others filled with pastry cream, jam, honey, pistachio cream... Sure, you can find sandwiches in an Italian café for breakfast, but they are not *that* common.

 PRONUNCIATION TEST!

How would you pronounce the Italian word **pistacchio**?

The correct pronunciation is *pee-stah-key-oh.*

If you are in a fancy café, or in one in the city center, please note that there could be a different price if you decide to have breakfast **al banco** — *at the counter* — or **al tavolo —** *at the table*. If you choose to sit at a table, you will probably have to pay more for the service.

Fair price for a coffee: 1.10–1.30€

Average price for a breakfast with coffee and croissant (al banco): 3–5€.

- **Brunch**   From 11:30 a.m.

Yes, brunch exists in Italy too, but it's a recent thing. This is the reason why you will be able to have a Sunday brunch in one of the main Italian cities but, if you are staying in a small town, it is quite unlikely that you will find a place serving brunch.

Average price for a brunch (depending on where you are): 10–20€

- **Pranzo** *Lunch*   Anytime from 12:30 to 2:00 p.m.

Italians generally have a late lunch, unless they have a set lunch break at work. If they are home, they eat around 1–1:30 p.m. For a quick lunch, we recommend going to a **bar**, where you will find not only tasty **panini** — sandwiches —but sometimes pasta dishes too. *Beware!* The word **panini** is in its plural form already. If you want just one, you should ask for a **panino.**

A typical Italian lunch during the week would include a big salad — **insalatona —** or a pasta dish — **un piatto di pasta —** or a sandwich. On the weekend, Italians may have a big family meal on Sundays, but it is not that common anymore. Big family meals are mainly held for festivities, such as Christmas.

One of the most common "mistakes" made by foreigners when having lunch in a restaurant is putting salad on top of pasta. If you do not want to get a funny look, please do not do that.

If you are in a restaurant, an Italian meal would always finish with an **espresso,** of course. The waiter — **il cameriere** — may also ask you if you want **un amaro** — *a digestive liqueur*. For example, the **limoncello** is considered an amaro and it's always served in a small glass. Usually 3–4€ is a fair price for an amaro.

- Average price for a panino: 4–6€

- Average price for a pasta dish: 7–12€

Merenda *Afternoon snack*   Anytime from 4:30 p.m.

We all know what you are thinking — **gelato!** Ice creams are probably the most common **merenda** in Italy, but only in summer. Some gelato shops even close in winter. What would you have when it gets cold outside, then? A **cioccolata calda** — a *hot chocolate* — for example. And why not, **con panna** — *with whipped cream*.

Average (fair) price for a small ice cream: 2.50–3.50€

- **Aperitivo** *Happy Hour*   From 6:30 to 8:00 p.m.

Is there anything better than enjoying a lovely **aperitivo** under the Italian sun? You can have an aperitivo in most Italian cafés, and sometimes even in restaurants. One of the most common cocktails Italians would have as a pre-dinner drink is the **spritz,** a wine-based cocktail, but you can have anything you want, from a soft drink to a glass of wine or **prosecco.** In general, the cocktail will come with chips and/or other snacks, like olives.

In some places, you can have an **apericena,** which is a combination of aperitivo and cena (dinner). In short, you order something to drink, and then you can eat as much as you want from the buffet.

Average price for an apericena: 15€

- **Cena** *Dinner*   Anytime from 8:00 p.m.

Yes, Italians usually have a late dinner. And consider that, the farther south you go, the later they eat. In fact, a dinner at eight would be considered an early dinner in some Italian regions. Please note that most restaurants — unless they are doing a **servizio continuato,** *meaning that they're open all day* — will not open before 7 p.m.

With regards to what Italians eat for dinner, for once, they have no "rules". They may have a pasta dish, meat or fish — **carne o pesce.** It is more common to eat a pizza for dinner rather than for lunch, though. If you *reeeeally* want a coffee after dinner — but you are scared to spend the whole night staring at the ceiling — go for a **decaffeinato,** or just **deca —** *a decaffeinated coffee.*

Average (fair) price for a pizza: 7–12€

 BEWARE! Never — *NEVER!* — use the verb **volere** — *to want* — in the present tense when asking for something because it is seen as very impolite. This is the reason why we decided to show you how to conjugate the verb volere in the conditional tense. *I would like* is always the best option.

io	**vorrei** *I would like*
tu	**vorresti** *you would like*
lui/lei/Lei	**vorrebbe** *he/she/it would like*
noi	**vorremmo** *we would like*
voi	**vorreste** *you would like*
loro	**vorrebbero** *they would like*

We will finish this chapter with some useful vocabulary and expressions related to food and restaurants:

antipasti	*appetizers*
primi	*first course (pasta dishes)*
secondi	*second course (meat, fish, or vegetarian dishes)*
contorni	*side dishes*
dolci	*desserts*
carta dei vini	*wine menu*
conto	*bill*
mancia	*tip (not mandatory, but always appreciated)*
prenotazione	*booking*
posso avere...?	*Can I have...?*
vorrei prenotare...	*I would like to book...*

✍ EXERCISES II

1. **Completa il dialogo.** *Complete the following dialogue.*

   Cameriere   Buongiorno, volete prendere qualcosa da bere?

   Tu   _____

   Cameriere   Perfetto. Ve le porto subito. Avete scelto gli antipasti?

   Tu   _____

   Cameriere   Ok. Prendete un primo?

   Tu   _____

   Cameriere   Bene. Gradite un secondo e un contorno?

   Tu   _____

   Cameriere   Benissimo. Vi ringrazio.

2. **Hai mai mangiato in un ristorante italiano?** *Have you ever eaten in an Italian restaurant? When? Where? What did you order? Write a short text in Italian.*

   _____

   _____

   _____

   _____

   _____

   _____

CHAPTER 3
TRAVELING

Traveling to a foreign country can be a stressful experience. This is the reason why we decided to help you by dedicating this chapter to the topic of traveling in Italy. Feeling nervous? **Non più!** *Not anymore!*

Let's start with the translation of the different means of transport and related places:

aereo	*plane*
aeroporto	*airport*
treno	*train*
stazione del treno	*train station*
taxi	*taxi*
autobus/bus	*bus*
fermata del bus	*bus stop*
tram	*tramway*
metropolitana	*subway*

When traveling by plane, of course, you must not forget your **passaporto** — *passport* — and your **biglietto** — *ticket*. Italian airports are not as big as the main American ones, for example, so you will probably not feel (*that*) overwhelmed. Do not forget to collect your **valigia / bagaglio** — *luggage* — though.

Other useful plane- and airport-related vocabulary:

bagaglio a mano	*hand luggage*
bagaglio in stiva	*checked baggage*
borsa	*bag*
zaino	*backpack*
volo	*flight*

fare il check-in	*to check in*
controlli di sicurezza	*security check*
carta di identità	*ID*
imbarcare	*to board*
decollare	*to take off*
atterrare	*to land*
ritiro bagagli	*baggage claim*
banco informazioni	*information desk*
cancellato	*cancelled (we hope you will never see this one)*
in ritardo	*delayed*
previsto alle...	*expected at...*

Once you get out of the airport, look for an *official* taxi. How can you recognize one? Well, in Italy, official taxis are white and they have a lit sign on the roof reading TAXI. In general, fares from/to airports are set. Please make sure to always have some cash with you. Nowadays, all taxis accept card payments, but **prevenire è sempre meglio che curare** — *better safe than sorry.*

One of the most stressful places when you're traveling around Italy is possibly a train station, especially a big one. They are quite chaotic, and you may find it hard to find your way and understand what you are supposed to do and where you should go.

First things first. Some train-related vocabulary:

biglietto sola andata	*one-way ticket*
biglietto andata e ritorno	*return ticket*
binario	*platform*
carrozza	*coach*
posto a sedere	*seat*
capotreno	*train manager*

One of the things you should pay attention to is the kind of train you are taking. In Italy, there are three main kinds of trains:

- **alta velocità (AV),** *high-speed trains:* they connect the biggest cities and are the fastest ones with the least stops. For example, to get from Rome to Florence will take one hour twenty/thirty minutes only. You will have a **posto assegnato** on these trains — *an assigned seat.*

- **regionali veloci** or **intercity**, *fast regional trains:* they connect smaller and bigger cities, but they are not as fast as the high-speed trains and do a lot of stops. As an example, if you take one of these trains to go from Rome to Florence it will take you four hours. Their abbreviation is **RV** or **IC.** You won't get an assigned seat on a RV train, but you'll get one on an IC one.

- **regionali**, *regional trains:* they connect small cities to other small ones or to the closest big city. For example, with a regional train, you can go from Rome to Viterbo — another city in the **Lazio** region — but you cannot go from Rome to Naples. Their abbreviation is **R** or **REG**. You do not get an assigned seat. You will have to fight for one — *just kidding.* Or maybe not.

Why did we mention the abbreviations? Well, take a look at this example of an Italian **tabellone** — *notice board* — below.

PARTENZE				10:40
PARTENZE	DESTINAZIONE	ORARIO	RIT	BIN
AV 9615	NAPOLI C.LE	10:05	50'	18
AV 9391	NAPOLI C.LE	10:10	40'	19
AV 9523	NAPOLI C.LE	10:25	45'	19
AV 9617	ROMA TERMINI	10:35	CANC	
AV 8907	ROMA TERMINI	10:40		18

In the first column, you can see the type of train, followed by its number. If you want to be sure that you are taking the right train, take a look at your train number on the screen at the platform.

Then you can see the destination — **destinazione** — the departure time — **orario** — and the indication of any delay expressed in minutes — **rit,** which stands for **ritardo.** Please note that, if the train is cancelled, this will be displayed.

Finally, you can see the platform number — **bin,** which stands for **binario.** The platform number is generally added a few minutes before the train arrives, so do not get nervous if you arrive at the train station and your platform number is still not shown.

Make sure that you are looking at the **PARTENZE** notice board — the *departures* one — and not the one with the **ARRIVI —** *arrivals*. It is a mistake we all have made. And still make sometimes. No matter where we come from.

Most importantly, do not forget to **convalidare —** *to validate —* your ticket before getting on the train. You will find the machines to validate your tickets at the platform. If you do not validate your ticket, and they check it on board, you might get **una multa —** *a fine.* Also, keep your tickets with you until you get out of the train station. If you are taking the bus or the tramway, you will have to validate your tickets on board as well.

You can buy your tickets directly at the train station, but, if you want to take a high-speed train, we recommend buying them online in advance, as the closer you get to the date, the more expensive the tickets become. No need to buy tickets in advance for the regional trains, as their price is set.

That's it! No need to get nervous again. **Adesso puoi partire in tutta tranquillità!** *Now you can leave with complete peace of mind.*

✒️ EXERCISES III

1. Aggiungi le traduzioni mancanti. *Add the missing translations in the table below.*

ITA	ENG
	bus stop
	luggage
	to land
ritardo	
	ticket
partenze	
	seat
	platform
carrozza	
decollare	

2. Ascolta l'audio e aggiungi le parole mancanti. *Listen to the audio and add the missing words.*

Ieri io e mia madre abbiamo preso _____ per andare in Germania a trovare una nostra

_____. Siamo arrivate _____ alle 8 e il nostro _____

era alle 12. Eravamo in grande _____, ma mia madre è sempre _____

quando dobbiamo _____. Siamo arrivate alle 14 e abbiamo recuperato subito i

_____. Poi abbiamo preso un taxi per il _____.

3. Racconta un viaggio che hai fatto. *Write a short text about a past trip.*

_____

_____

_____

_____

_____

CHAPTER 4
SENDING AN EMAIL

Sending an email may seem quite an easy thing to do, but that is not always the case, especially when you are emailing someone that you do not know or to make a request in a different language.

If you think about it, when we write an email in English, there are some fixed expressions.

So, with this chapter, we would like to teach you how to structure an email in Italian. As you may guess, it is not complicated: you just need to learn a few expressions so that your email sounds natural and appropriate in Italian.

Let us show you an example of a standard email in Italian to book a hotel room:

Buongiorno / Buonasera,

Mi chiamo Lucia e vorrei prenotare una camera doppia nella vostra struttura dal 13 al 17 luglio (4 notti). Avete disponibilità in quelle date? Vorrei anche qualche informazione sui prezzi e sui servizi aggiuntivi (colazione, piscina, ecc.).

Vi ringrazio in anticipo,
Cordiali saluti,
Lucia Pistri

Translation

Good morning / Good evening,

My name is Lucia and I would like to book a double room in your hotel from July 13 to July 17 (4 nights). Do you have any availability on those dates? I would also like some information on the prices and additional services (breakfast, swimming pool, etc.).

Thanks in advance,
Best regards,
Lucia Pistri

The first thing you should notice is that we have always used the verb **volere** conjugated in the conditional tense — **vorrei.** As previously mentioned, it is important to use it in this tense to sound polite.

To start an email, in Italian, it is quite unusual to use **caro / cara —** *dear* — unless you already know the person to whom you are sending the email to. The same applies to **ciao**, which is very informal and should not be used unless you already know the recipient.

You can see that, when addressing the recipient, we used *you* — plural — as the subject pronoun, as in **avete disponibilità**. If you remember, we said that whenever you need to be formal, you should use *she* — **Lei** — as the subject pronoun. When you are emailing a hotel, it is very common to use **voi** as the subject, because it is as if you were addressing all the people working there. However, when you receive an answer from one of the employees, you can start using **Lei** as the subject pronoun, because now you are writing to *that* person only.

Once you write the body of an email, it is common to thank the recipient in advance. *In advance for what*, you may ask. Well, for their reply. This is a polite way to let the other person know that you are expecting an answer. Do not literally translate the expression *I am looking forward to hearing from you* — which would be **non vedo l'ora di sentirti —** because it sounds very weird — and almost inappropriate! — unless you are emailing/texting a friend.

Cordiali saluti is the equivalent of *best regards*. Another option is **cordialmente**. It is a very formal expression, though, and you should not use it with friends, family etc.

Now that you know how to write an email in Italian, it is time to introduce some useful email-related vocabulary:

allegato	*attachment*	**firmare**	*to sign*
allegare	*to attach (just for emails)*	**risposta**	*reply/answer*
inviare	*to send*	**domanda**	*question*
ricevere	*to receive*	**a presto**	*see you soon*
firma	*signature*	**avrei bisogno di...**	*I would need...*

If you send an email, and you do not receive an answer after 3–4 working days, feel free to send another one, or to give them a call to let them know that you sent an email, but received no answer. Stalking your recipient via email/phone to try to get an answer to an important email you sent is not a crime.

✏️ EXERCISES IV

1. **Scrivi la tua prima e-mail in italiano.** *Write your first email in Italian to a hotel. Email them to ask about their availability, and other information on the hotel and what they are offering.*

_____

_____

_____

_____

_____

2. **Scrivi la tua seconda e-mail in italiano!** *Now write your second email in Italian, this time to someone you know. For example, you are emailing them to send them the tickets to go to a concert together.*

_____

_____

_____

_____

_____

🎧 READING COMPREHENSION

Before finishing this book, there is a final challenge for you to face: *your first reading comprehension exercise!*

Do not feel disappointed when you start reading the following text, though. One thing is sure: there will be words that you do not know, and there will be sentences that you will not be able to translate right away. And it is perfectly *normal*. You will find the translation of the text at the end of the book, but try not to look at it before finishing the reading comprehension exercises.

We suggest reading the text a first time — without stress. Try to get a sense of it, to understand what it is about. Then read it a second time, and now pay more attention to the details. If there are certain words that you do not know, and that are preventing you from understanding the meaning of a sentence, look them up in the dictionary. Remember: A dictionary is always a trustworthy friend.

La nostra prima vacanza a Roma

L'anno scorso io e mia moglie siamo andati a Roma per la prima volta in vita nostra! I miei suoceri ci hanno offerto i biglietti aerei come regalo per il nostro quindicesimo anniversario. Non vedevamo l'ora di partire.

Abbiamo passato una settimana a Roma, e abbiamo cercato di vedere il più possibile. Ovviamente, non siamo riusciti a fare tutto. Abbiamo visitato i musei principali e anche i siti archeologici della città... che meraviglia!

Alloggiavamo in un hotel in centro e ci svegliavamo ogni mattina alle sette e mezzo per goderci la città quando ancora era poco affollata. Tornavamo direttamente dopo cena, stanchissimi!

Facevamo colazione in un bar vicino all'hotel. Facevano un caffè ottimo! Per pranzo o ci fermavamo in una trattoria locale, o prendevamo un panino al volo. Per cena, invece, preferivamo sederci in un buon ristorante.

Il piatto che mi è piaciuto di più è probabilmente la pasta alla carbonara. Semplice, ma buonissima. Il cuoco di una trattoria mi ha dato la ricetta, che mi ha sorpreso perché è davvero semplice. Il sugo della pasta è fatto con uova (soprattutto il tuorlo, che è la parte gialla), pepe, formaggio e guanciale croccante. Deliziosa.

Abbiamo comprato qualche souvenir per i nostri parenti e amici. Volevo prendere anche altre cose, ma la nostra valigia pesava già troppo. Sono dei piccoli regali, ma, come dicono gli Italiani, *è il pensiero che conta.*

È stata una settimana indimenticabile. La prossima volta vorrei visitare anche altre città italiane, e magari anche andare in Sicilia in estate, anche se farà molto caldo. I miei amici mi hanno detto che Bologna è una città molto carina. Chissà, forse andremo lì per le prossime vacanze.

✏️ EXERCISES

Rispondi alle seguenti domande. *Answer the following questions about the text you have just read. The translation of the questions is at the end of the book. No cheating, though!*

- Dove sono andati in vacanza?

  _____

- Quanti giorni sono rimasti in città?

  _____

- A che ora si svegliavano la mattina?

  _____

- Quali sono gli ingredienti della pasta alla carbonara?

  _____

- Dove andranno per le prossime vacanze?

  _____

- Sei mai stato/a in Italia? Se sì, quando e dove? Se no, ti piacerebbe andare?

  _____

- Dove andrai per le prossime vacanze?

  _____

⚠ FALSE FRIENDS

You thought that this book was over, didn't you? Well, to be honest, it is. However, before leaving you, we thought that it would be fun to add a short list of the most common false friends in Italian. Once you know them, you can do your best to avoid any possible **figuraccia** — *gaffe*.

addetto	*assigned (addicted* is **dipendente**)
allegato	*attachment (allegation* is **accusa**)
annoiarsi	*to get bored (to annoy* is **infastidire**)
argomento	*topic (argument* is **litigio** or **discussione**)
attendere	*to wait (to attend* is **partecipare**)
attualmente	*recently (actually* is **a dire il vero**)
bravo	*good, clever (brave* is **coraggioso**)
calamita	*magnet (calamity* is **calamità**)
caldo	*hot (cold* is **freddo**!)
camera	*room (camera* is **macchina fotografica, fotocamera**)
cantina	*cellar (canteen* is **mensa**)
collera	*rage* (no diseases involved)
confrontare	*to compare (to confront* is **affrontare**)
conveniente	*good value (convenient* is **comodo**)
delusione	*disappointment (delusion* is **illusione**)

educazione	*politeness (education* is **istruzione**)
estate	*summer (estate* is **proprietà**)
fattoria	*farm (factory* is **fabbrica**)
grosso	*big (gross* is **disgustoso**)
libreria	*bookshop (library* is **biblioteca**)
magazzino	*warehouse (magazine* is **rivista**)
morbido	*soft (morbid* is **morboso**)
parenti	*relatives (parents* is **genitori**)
pretendere	*to demand (to pretend* is **fingere**)
ricordo	*a memory (record* is **registrare**)
rumore	*noise (rumour* is **pettegolezzo**)
stampa	*print (stamp* is **francobollo**)

CONCLUSION

Ce l'hai fatta! *You made it!*

You have reached the end of this book on Italian grammar. And yes, this is the end for real. We really hope that you enjoyed this journey into the Italian language, and that now you feel more motivated than ever to continue. In fact, you have just taken the first steps — a little bit like getting your first Karate belts. Now it is time to keep on training to get the next one.

We know that learning a new language is not easy, but **guardati indietro** — *look behind you*. You have learned so much already! Come on, you even faced the articulated prepositions. You won. You *nailed* it.

Even if you did not ask for it, we decided to give you a piece of advice to navigate this learning experience:

- The most important thing, when learning a new language, is *consistency*. You have finished this book, but do not break the bond with the Italian language. Of course, if you need it, take a (short) break. But do not stop including this new language in your daily routine. Even ten minutes per day are enough.

- Take those ten minutes to watch a video in Italian, for example. Listen to an Italian song, read an article in Italian. Start watching a TV series in Italian. Buy the other two books your author wrote on the Italian language. **Tutto conta,** *everything counts*. Use every tool you can find to include the Italian language in your everyday life. And remember that we are in the 21st century. We have *plenty* of tools, if we want to use them.

- Most importantly, do not focus on one skill only. You have to practice *all of them*. That means that you should read, listen, speak, and write in Italian. Some people find that the hardest skill is listening, others think that speaking is the most difficult when it comes to learning a new language. Everyone is different, but that does not mean that you should focus on the thing that you find the easiest. It is quite the opposite. Remember: *No pain, no gain!*

- Do not be afraid to speak in Italian, and use every single opportunity to practice. You will make mistakes — because let's be honest, **farai degli errori**, and it is perfectly normal. Be kind to yourself and remember that you are speaking in a foreign language — basically, you are a superhero already! It will get better and better with practice.

- Learning a new language requires *time*. You cannot expect to become fluent in a couple of months, and not even in a year. That means one thing only: you must be *patient*. In fact, right now, you are building the foundation of your Italian villa. You want to build a strong one, if you want it to be able to support the walls, and we know that you do not want your nice house to collapse after a few months. This is the reason why,, when it comes to learning a new language, you do not need to rush.

- As the Italians say, **la fretta è cattiva consigliera** — meaning that *haste is a poor advisor*, and this saying applies to learning new languages as well. It is better to learn little by little than a massive full immersion to try to speed up the process.

Do you know what Michelangelo once said? **Sto ancora imparando** — *I am still learning*. So keep on learning with us!

Grazie mille per averci scelto. A presto!

Thank you so much for choosing us. See you soon!

IRREGULAR VERBS IN THE PRESENT TENSE

	ANDARE *to leave*	VENIRE *to come*	STARE *to stay*
io	vado	vengo	sto
tu	vai	vieni	stai
lui/lei/lei	va	viene	sta
noi	andiamo	veniamo	stiamo
voi	andate	venite	state
loro	vanno	vengono	stanno

	FARE *to do*	DARE *to give*	DIRE *to say*
io	faccio	do	dico
tu	fai	dai	dici
lui/lei/Lei	fa	dà	dice
noi	facciamo	diamo	diciamo
voi	fate	date	dite
loro	fanno	danno	dicono

	USCIRE *to go out*	TENERE *to keep*	SCEGLIERE *to choose*
io	esco	tengo	scelgo
tu	esci	tieni	scegli
lui/lei/Lei	esce	tiene	sceglie

noi	usciamo	teniamo	scegliamo
voi	uscite	tenete	scegliete
loro	escono	tengono	scelgono

	SALIRE *to go up*	**RIUSCIRE** *to manage to do something*	**BERE** *to drink*
io	salgo	riesco	bevo
tu	sali	riesci	bevi
lui/lei/Lei	sale	riesce	beve
noi	saliamo	riusciamo	beviamo
voi	salite	riuscite	bevete
loro	salgono	riescono	bevono

	POTERE *to be able to – can*	**SAPERE** *to know*	**VOLERE** *to want*
io	posso	so	voglio
tu	puoi	sai	vuoi
lui/lei/Lei	può	sa	vuole
noi	possiamo	sappiamo	vogliamo
voi	potete	sapete	volete
loro	possono	sanno	vogliono

REFLEXIVE VERBS

abituarsi a	*to get used to*	**scusarsi**	*to apologize*
addormentarsi	*to fall asleep*	**sdraiarsi**	*to lie down*
alzarsi	*to get up*	**sentirsi**	*to feel*
annoiarsi	*to get bored*	**svegliarsi**	*to wake up*
arrabbiarsi	*to get angry*	**trovarsi**	*to be located*
avvicinarsi	*to get closer*	**vestirsi**	*to get dressed*
cambiarsi	*to change clothes*		
chiamarsi	*to be named*		
divertirsi	*to have fun*		
esprimersi	*to express oneself*		
farsi la doccia	*to have a shower*		
fermarsi	*to stop*		
incontrarsi	*to meet*		
lamentarsi	*to complain*		
lavarsi	*to wash oneself*		
pettinarsi	*to comb one's hair*		
portarsi dietro	*to carry around*		
preoccuparsi	*to worry*		
prepararsi	*to get ready*		
presentarsi	*to introduce oneself*		
ricordarsi di	*to remember*		
riposarsi	*to rest*		
sbrigarsi	*to hurry*		

RECIPROCAL VERBS

abbracciarsi	*to hug each other*
aiutarsi	*to help each other*
amarsi	*to love each other*
baciarsi	*to kiss each other*
conoscersi	*to know each other*
incontrarsi	*to meet each other*
innamorarsi	*to fall in love with each other*
insultarsi	*to insult each other*
odiarsi	*to hate each other*
parlarsi	*to talk to each other*
rispettarsi	*to respect each other*
riunirsi	*to gather / get together*
salutarsi	*to greet each other*
scriversi	*to write to each other*
sposarsi	*to get married*
telefonarsi	*to call each other*
vedersi	*to see each other*

IRREGULAR VERBS IN THE PAST PARTICIPLE

INFINITIVE	PAST PARTICIPLE
Aprire *(to open)*	Aperto *(opened)*
Accendere *(to switch on)*	Acceso *(switched on)*
Bere *(to drink)*	Bevuto *(drunk)*
Chiedere *(to ask)*	Chiesto *(asked)*
Chiudere *(to close)*	Chiuso *(closed)*
Correre *(to run)*	Corso *(run)*
Decidere *(to decide)*	Deciso *(decided)*
Dire *(to say/tell)*	Detto *(said/told)*
Dividere *(to divide)*	Diviso *(divided)*
Essere *(to be)*	Stato *(been)*
Fare *(to do/make)*	Fatto *(done/made)*
Leggere *(to read)*	Letto *(read)*
Mettere *(to put)*	Messo *(put)*
Nascere *(to be born)*	Nato *(born)*
Perdere *(to lose)*	Perso *(lost)*
Piangere *(to cry)*	Pianto *(cried)*
Prendere *(to take)*	Preso *(taken)*
Ridere *(to laugh)*	Riso *(laughed)*

Rimanere *(to stay)*	Rimasto *(stayed)*
Rispondere *(to answer)*	Risposto *(answered)*
Scegliere *(to choose)*	Scelto *(chosen)*
Scendere *(to get off)*	Sceso *(got off)*
Scoprire *(to find out)*	Scoperto *(found out)*
Scrivere *(to write)*	Scritto *(written)*
Spegnere *(to switch off)*	Spento *(switched off)*
Spendere *(to spend – money)*	Speso *(spent)*
Succedere *(to happen)*	Successo *(happened)*
Togliere *(to take off)*	Tolto *(taken off)*
Tradurre *(to translate)*	Tradotto *(translated)*
Vedere *(to see)*	Visto *(seen)*
Venire *(to come)*	Venuto *(come)*
Vivere *(to live)*	Vissuto *(lived)*
Vincere *(to win)*	Vinto *(won)*

ANSWER KEY

UNIT 1

Exercises I

1)
- lampadina   lahm-pah-de-nah
- televisione   teh-leh-ve-sea-oh-neh
- cuscino   coo-she-noh
- zanzara   dzahn-dzah-rah
- radio   rah-de-oh
- albero   ahl-beh-roh
- verdure   vehr-doo-reh
- gnomo   ñoh-moh

2)
- ventilatore
- inverno
- laggiù
- caminetto
- librerie
- scimmia
- pugno
- collina
- sogliola

Exercises II

1)

ENGLISH	ITALIANO
I	io
you	tu
he/she	lui/lei
we	noi
you (pl)	voi
they	loro

2)
- saltare   salt-   *to jump*
- capirsi   cap-   *to understand each other*
- lanciare   lanci-   *to throw*
- scegliere   scegli-   *to choose*
- comprare   compr-   *to buy*
- radere   rad-   *to shave*
- salutare   salut-   *to greet*
- condire   cond-   *to season*
- lamentarsi   lament-   *to complain*

Exercises III

1) Mi chiamo Marco e sono un <u>insegnante</u> di <u>francese</u>. Lavoro al <u>liceo</u> da dieci <u>anni</u>. Insegnare è la <u>passione</u> della mia <u>vita</u>, anche se da <u>bambino</u> sognavo di diventare un <u>attore</u> famoso! Nel mio <u>tempo</u> libero mi piace viaggiare ed esplorare dei <u>posti</u> nuovi, visitare <u>musei</u>, e andare ai <u>concerti</u>.

My name is Marco and I am a French teacher. I have been working in a high school for ten years. Teaching is my life's passion, even if I dreamed of becoming a famous actor when I was a child! In my free time, I like traveling and exploring new places, visiting museums, and going to concerts.

2)

NOME	MASCHILE	FEMMINILE	SINGOLARE	PLURALE
tavolo	X		X	
piedi	X			X
salotto	X		X	
zebra		X	X	
zie		X		X
scanner	X		X	X
martedì	X		X	

vanità		X	X	
biglie		X		X
cane	X		X	

Exercises IV

1) *The exercise involves the ability to describe oneself based on the information learned so far.*

2)

MS	FS	MP	FP
verde	verde	verdi	verdi
brutto	brutta	brutti	brutte
tranquillo	tranquilla	tranquilli	tranquille
bravo	brava	bravi	brave

Exercises V

1) Mio fratello ha avuto il suo ultimo esame ieri. Si è svegliato molto presto per andare all'università con il bus ed è arrivato con trenta minuti di anticipo! Gli esami lo rendono sempre molto nervoso. Alla fine è andato benissimo! È tornato a casa contento e soddisfatto di se stesso.

My brother had his last exam yesterday. He woke up very early to go to the university by bus and arrived thirty minutes early! Exams always make him very nervous. In the end, it went great! He came back home happy and proud of himself.

2)

AGGETTIVO	AVVERBIO
rapido	rapidamente
beato	beatamente
leale	lealmente
dolce	dolcemente
regolare	regolarmente

Exercises VI

1)
- Comprerai presto casa?
- Sono stato al supermercato.
- Abbiamo cantato tutti insieme.
- Non si sono dimenticati la loro promessa.
- Vieni anche tu in vacanza?
- Tua sorella non capisce questo esercizio.
- Giochiamo a scacchi?

2)
- Siamo andati al mare lo scorso fine settimana. *We went to the seaside last weekend.*
  Non siamo andati al mare lo scorso fine settimana. (N)

- Prendo una bibita fresca? *Do I get a fresh drink?*
  Prendo una bibita fresca. (A)

- Non mangia i latticini. *He/She doesn't eat dairy products.*
  Mangia i latticini? (?)

- Marco parte ogni estate con i suoi amici. *Marco goes away every summer with his friends.*
  Marco non parte ogni estate con i suoi amici. (N)

- Hai visto la luna stasera? *Have you seen the moon tonight?*
  Hai visto la luna stasera. (A)

- Preferiscono il mare alla piscina. *They prefer the sea to the swimming pool.*
  Preferiscono il mare alla piscina? (?)

UNIT 2

Exercises I

1)
·	35	trentacinque
·	72	settantadue
·	33	trentatré
·	91	novantuno
·	58	cinquantotto
·	3	tre
·	246	duecentoquarantasei
·	999	novecentonovantanove
·	1320	milletrecentoventi
·	9021	novemilaventuno

2) *The exercise involves the ability to answer some questions based on the information learned so far.*

Exercises II

1)
·	42th	quarantaduesimo	MS
·	13th	tredicesimi	MP
·	33th	trentatreesima	FS
·	191th	centonovantunesime	FP
·	1st	primi	MP
·	9th	none	FP
·	71st	settantunesimo	MS
·	10th	decima	FS

2) Ieri ho partecipato alla mia prima gara di scherma! È stata un'esperienza bellissima. Mi allenavo da cinque anni per questo momento. Non sono arrivato primo, ma nono. Sono stato comunque molto orgoglioso del mio risultato. C'erano quaranta atleti in gara!

Yesterday I took part in my first fencing competition! It has been a wonderful experience. I had been training for five years for this moment. I did not come first, but ninth. I am still very proud of my result. There were forty athletes in the competition!

1)

SING.	PLUR.
IL	I
LO	GLI
LA	LE
L'	GLI/LE

2)
- la barca (f. sing.)
- il divano (m. sing.)
- gli angoli (m. plur.)
- l'aereo (m. sing.)
- l'epoca (f. sing.)

- le vittorie (f. plur.)
- lo scoglio (m. sing.)
- gli zuccheri (m. plur.)
- le artiste (f. plur.)

3)
- un aperitivo (m.)
- un fiore (m.)
- una malattia (f.)
- un'esperienza (f.)
- uno stadio (m.)

Exercises IV

1)

	MS	FS	MP	FP
my	mio	mia	miei	mie
your	tuo	tua	tuoi	tue
his/her/its	suo	sua	suoi	sue

our	**nostro**	**nostra**	**nostri**	**nostre**
your	**vostro**	**vostra**	**vostri**	**vostre**
their	**loro**	**loro**	**loro**	**loro**

2)
- My brother — mio fratello
- Their sons — i loro figli
- Our father — nostro padre
- Your niece — tua nipote/vostra nipote
- My sisters — le mie sorelle
- His aunt — sua zia
- Their uncles — i loro zii
- Your cousin — tuo cugino/tua cugina/vostro cugino/vostra cugina

3) La mia famiglia è molto grande! Ho tre fratelli e due sorelle, sette zii e quattordici cugini. Ci riuniamo sempre per Natale e ci divertiamo sempre tantissimo. I miei genitori hanno lavorato sodo per supportarci, e ora spero di poter fare lo stesso con loro.

Translation:

My family is very big! I have got three brothers and two sisters, seven uncles, and fourteen cousins. We always gather for Christmas, and we always have so much fun. My parents worked hard to support us, and now I hope to do the same for them.

Exercises V

1)
- mi — REF, DP, IP
- lui — SP
- vi — REF, DP, IP
- le — IP
- la — DP
- che — RP
- si — REF
- lo — DP

2) Ti presento un amico che conosco da una vita, Luca! L'ho conosciuto durante una vacanza quando eravamo giovani. Da allora ci siamo visti molte volte. Lui è un tipo molto estroverso, io, invece, sono molto timido. Ti ho già parlato di sua moglie, Francesca, che lavora con lui? Vorrei darle un regalo per il suo compleanno.

Translation

I want to introduce a friend that I have known all my life, Luca! I met him during a holiday when we were young. Since then, we have seen each other several times. He is very outgoing, while I am very shy. Have I talked to you about his wife, Francesca, who works with him? I would like to give her a birthday present.

Exercises VI

1)

	IL	LO	LA	L'	I	GLI	LE
DI	del	dello	della	dell'	dei	degli	delle
A	al	allo	alla	all'	ai	agli	alle
DA	dal	dallo	dalla	dall'	dai	dagli	dalle
IN	nel	nello	nella	nell'	nei	negli	nelle
CON	con il	con lo	con la	con l'	con i	con gli	con le
SU	sul	sullo	sulla	sull'	sui	sugli	sulle
PER	per il	per lo	per la	per l'	per i	per gli	per le
TRA/FRA	tra il	tra lo	tra la	tra l'	tra i	tra gli	tra le

2) · Francesca viene **dall'**Italia.
Francesca comes from Italy.

· **Nella** sua città ci sono pochi supermercati.
In his/her city, there are few supermarkets.

· Dove stai andando? **Alla** stazione!
Where are you going? To the train station!

· La finestra è **tra la** televisione e la radio.
The window is between the TV and the radio.

· Mi hanno parlato bene **del** professore.
They spoke well about the professor.

· Mio padre è seduto **sulla** sedia.
My father is sitting on the chair.

· Vi stavamo aspettando **con la** cena pronta!
We were waiting for you with the dinner ready!

· È molto dinamico **per la** sua età.
He is very active for his age.

UNIT 3

Exercises I

1) · partire **part-** *to leave*
   · credere **cred-** *to believe*
   · comprare **compr-** *to buy*
   · vincere **vinc-** *to win*
   · prendere **prend-** *to take*
   · scegliere **scegli-** *to choose*
   · mentire **ment-** *to lie*

2)

	AMARE *to love*	**PIANGERE** *to cry*	**FINIRE** *to finish*
io	amo	piango	finisco
tu	ami	piangi	finisci
lui/lei/Lei	ama	piange	finisce
noi	amiamo	piangiamo	finiamo
voi	amate	piangete	finite
loro	amano	piangono	finiscono

3) · **Vado** sempre al mare a settembre. (andare, io)
     I always go to the seaside in September.

   · **Cucina** le migliori torte del mondo! (cucinare, lei)
     She makes the best cakes in the world!

   · Quando **parti** per l'Africa? (partire, tu)
     When do you leave for Africa?

- **Puliscono** casa tutti i giorni. (pulire, loro)
  They clean their house every day.

- **Veniamo** dagli Stati Uniti. (venire, noi)
  We come from the United States.

- Sig. Rossi, mi **scrive** il suo indirizzo, per favore? (scrivere, Lei)
  Mister Rossi, could you write your address for me?

Exercises II

1) to talk to each other = parlarsi
to have a shower = farsi la doccia
to hug each other = abbracciarsi
to get angry = arrabbiarsi
to meet = incontrarsi

to kiss each other = baciarsi
to stop = fermarsi
to call each other = telefonarsi
to get bored = annoiarsi

2) *The exercise involves the ability to build simple sentences based on the information learned so far.*

Exercises III

1)
prendere	A	*to take*
venire	E	*to come*
svegliarsi	E	*to wake up*
cantare	A	*to sing*
vedere	A	*to see*
stare	E	*to stay*
avvicinarsi	E	*to get closer*
aprire	A	*to open*

2)
prendere	**preso**
venire	**venuto**
svegliarsi	**svegliato**
cantare	**cantato**
vedere	**visto**
stare	**stato**
avvicinarsi	**avvicinato**
aprire	**aperto**

3) Dieci anni fa, sono partito per la Germania per fare un semestre all'estero. È stata un'esperienza incredibile. Non solo ho esplorato un'altra università e ho imparato un'altra lingua, ma ho incontrato persone di tutto il mondo, che poi sono diventate miei amici. Ho visitato delle città magnifiche e non mi sono pentito per niente della mia scelta!

Exercises IV

1)

	PAGARE *to pay*	VENDERE *to sell*	COSTRUIRE *to build*
io	pagavo	vendevo	costruivo
tu	pagavi	vendevi	costruivi
lui/lei/Lei	pagava	vendeva	costruiva
noi	pagavamo	vendevamo	costruivamo
voi	pagavate	vendevate	costruivate
loro	pagavano	vendevano	costruivano

2)
- Ieri **ho comprato** una nuova bicicletta. (comprare, io)
- I cugini **giocavano** sempre insieme. (giocare, loro)
- **Sei** mai **stato** a Madrid? (essere, tu)
- **Abbiamo scoperto** che quest'anno si licenzieranno. (noi, scoprire)
- Da piccolo **aveva** tantissimi amici a scuola. (avere, lui)
- Mentre **mangiavamo**, **abbiamo ricevuto** una chiamata. (mangiare-ricevere, noi).

3) *The exercise involves the ability to build simple sentences with the imperfect tense based on the information learned so far.*

UNIT 4

Exercises I

1)

ENG	ITA
Tuesday	**martedì**
Sunday	**domenica**
March	**marzo**
Wednesday	**mercoledì**
June	**giugno**
October	**ottobre**
August	**agosto**
July	**luglio**
Thursday	**giovedì**
Saturday	**sabato**
January	**gennaio**

2) *The exercise involves the ability to build simple sentences based on the information learned so far.*

Exercises II

1)
- 12:00   **sono le dodici (in punto) / è mezzogiorno**
- 13:15   **sono le tredici e quindici / è l'una e un quarto**
- 4:30   **sono le quattro e trenta / sono le quattro e mezzo**
- 18:25   **sono le diciotto e venticinque / sono le sei e venticinque**
- 22:45   **sono le ventidue e quarantacinque / sono le undici meno un quarto**
- 00:00   **è mezzanotte**
- 7:55   **sono le sette e cinquantacinque / sono le otto meno cinque**
- 19:00   **sono le diciannove (in punto) / sono le sette**

2) *The exercise involves the ability to build simple sentences based on the information learned so far.*

Exercises III

1) *The exercise involves the ability to build simple sentences based on the information learned so far.*

2) Una delle cose che ci piace di più è suonare il sax. Adoriamo la musica jazz e i cantanti blues. Abbiamo un gruppo e ci incontriamo ogni settimana per suonare insieme. La prossima settimana abbiamo il nostro primo concerto! Siamo molto emozionati.

Translation

One of the things we like the most is playing the sax. We love jazz music and blues singers. We have a band and we meet every week to play together. Next week we have our first concert! We are very excited.

Exercises IV

1)

	CONTROLLARE *to check*	NEGARE *to deny*	SUGGERIRE *to suggest*
io	controllerò	negherò	suggerirò
tu	controllerai	negherai	suggerirai
lui/lei/Lei	controllerà	negherà	suggerirà
noi	controlleremo	negheremo	suggeriremo
voi	controllerete	negherete	suggerirete
loro	controlleranno	negheranno	suggeriranno

2) *The exercise involves the ability to build simple sentences based on the information learned so far.*

UNIT 5

Exercises I

1)

parrucchiere	hairdresser's
macelleria	butcher's
edicola	newsstand
gioielleria	jewelry store
pescheria	fish shop
negozio di scarpe	shoe store
forno	bakery

2) Oggi io e le mie amiche siamo andate a fare shopping! Avevo bisogno di un paio nuovo di scarpe, quindi quella è stata la nostra prima tappa. Poi una mia amica voleva comprare una rivista all'edicola. Ho comprato anche il giornale per mia madre. Avevamo fame e per la merenda siamo andate al forno vicino al centro commerciale. È il migliore della città.

Translation

Today, my friends and I went shopping! I needed a new pair of shoes, so that was our first stop. A friend of mine wanted to buy a magazine at the newsstand. I bought the newspaper for my mother too. We were hungry and we went to the bakery near the mall for a snack. It is the best one in town!

Exercises II

1) Waiter   Good morning, would you like something to drink?

You   _____

Waiter   Perfect. I will bring them right away. Have you chosen any appetizers?

You   _____

Waiter   Okay. Will you have a first course?

You   _____

Waiter	Okay. Would you like a second course and a side dish?
You	_____
Waiter	Perfect. Thank you.

The exercise involves the ability to build simple sentences based on the information learned so far.

2) *The exercise involves the ability to build simple sentences based on the information learned so far.*

Exercises III

1)

ITA	ENG
fermata del bus	*bus stop*
bagaglio / valigia	*luggage*
atterrare	*to land*
ritardo	*delay*
biglietto	*ticket*
partenze	*departures*
posto	*seat*
binario	*platform*
carrozza	*coach*
decollare	*to take off*

2) Ieri io e mia madre abbiamo preso l'aereo per andare in Germania a trovare una nostra amica. Siamo arrivate in aeroporto alle 8 e il nostro volo era alle 12. Eravamo in grande anticipo, ma mia madre è sempre stressata quando dobbiamo viaggiare. Siamo arrivate alle 14 e abbiamo recuperato subito i bagagli. Poi abbiamo preso un taxi per il centro città.

Translation

Yesterday, my mother and I took the plane to go to Germany to visit a friend of ours. We arrived at the airport at 8, and our flight was at 12. We were very early, but my mother is always stressed when we have to travel. We arrived at 2 p.m. and got our luggage immediately. Then we took a taxi for the city center.

3) *The exercise involves the ability to build simple sentences based on the information learned so far.*

Exercises IV

1) *The exercise involves the ability to build simple sentences based on the information learned so far.*

2) *The exercise involves the ability to build simple sentences based on the information learned so far.*

READING COMPREHENSION

Translation

Our first holiday in Rome

Last year my wife and I went to Rome for the first time in our lives! My in-laws gave us the plane tickets as a gift for our fifteenth anniversary. We were looking forward to going there.

We spent a week in Rome, and we tried to see as much as possible. Of course, we did not manage to see everything. We visited the main museums and the archaeological sites of the city... how wonderful!

We were staying in a hotel in the city center and we woke up every morning at half past seven to enjoy the city when it was not too crowded. We came back to the hotel after dinner, and we were extremely tired!

We had breakfast in a café near the hotel. Their coffee was amazing! For lunch, we stopped at a local *trattoria* or took a sandwich on the fly. For dinner, we preferred sitting in a good restaurant.

The dish I liked the most is probably *pasta alla carbonara*. A simple dish, but very tasty. The chef of a trattoria gave me the recipe, which surprised me because it is really simple. The pasta sauce is made with eggs (especially with the yolk, which is the yellow part), pepper, cheese, and crispy bacon. Delicious.

We bought a few souvenirs for our friends and family. I wanted to take other things too, but our luggage was too heavy already. They are small gifts, but, as the Italians say, it is the thought that counts.

It has been an unforgettable week. Next time, I would like to visit other Italian cities, and maybe go to Sicily in summer, even if it is going to be very hot. My friends told me that Bologna is a very nice city. Who knows, maybe we will go there for our next holiday.

Exercises

Rispondi alle seguenti domande. *Answer the following questions about the text you have just read.*

- Dove sono andati in vacanza?
  Where did they go on holiday?
  A Roma.

- Quanti giorni sono rimasti in città?
  How long did they stay in the city?
  Una settimana, quindi sette giorni.

- A che ora si svegliavano la mattina?
  What time did they wake up in the morning?
  Alle sette e mezzo.

- Quali sono gli ingredienti della pasta alla carbonara?
  What are the ingredients of the pasta alla carbonara?
  Uova (e in particolare il tuorlo), pepe, formaggio, e guanciale croccante.

- Dove andranno per le prossime vacanze?
  Where will they go for their next holidays?
  A loro piacerebbe tornare in Italia e visitare altre città, forse la Sicilia in estate. O anche Bologna.

- Sei mai stato/a in Italia? Se sì, quando e dove? Se no, ti piacerebbe andare?
  Have you ever been to Italy? If so, when and where? If not, would you like to go there?

- Dove andrai per le prossime vacanze?
  Where will you go on your next holiday?

The last two questions involve the ability to answer based on the information learned so far.

MORE BOOKS BY LINGO MASTERY

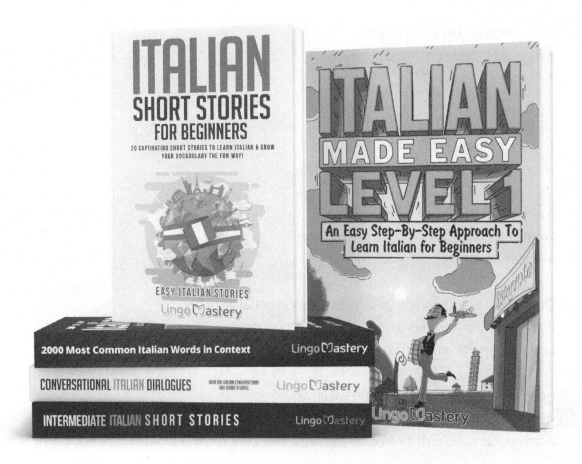

We are not done teaching you Italian until you're fluent!

Here are some other titles you might find useful in your journey of mastering Italian:

✓ Italian Short Stories for Beginners

✓ Intermediate Italian Short Stories

✓ 2000 Most Common Italian Words in Context

✓ Conversational Italian Dialogues

But we have many more!

Check out all of our titles at **www.lingomastery.com/italian**

Made in United States
Orlando, FL
10 December 2024

55345102R00102